LEAVING CULTS: THE DYNAMICS OF DEFECTION

by

Stuart A. Wright

Department of Sociology
Lamar University

91-174

Society for the Scientific Study of Religion
Monograph Series, Washington, D.C.
ISBN 0-932566-06-5

This book contains some materials previously published in Stuart A. Wright, "Defection from New Religious Movements: A Test of Some Theoretical Propositions," in David G. Bromley and James T. Richardson (eds.), *The Brainwashing/Deprogramming Controversy* (NY: Edwin Mellen); Stuart A. Wright, "Post-Involvement Attitudes of Voluntary Defectors from Controversial New Religious Movements," *Journal for the Scientific Study of Religion* 23: 172-182; Stuart A. Wright, "Dyadic Intimacy and Social Control in Three Cult Movements," *Sociological Analysis* 47: 137-150; and are used here with permission.

Library of Congress Number: 87-61788
International Standard Book Number: 0-932566-06-5

Editor's Introduction

The study of religion has engendered a wide range of investigations, some scholastic to the point of obfuscation, others, so inclined to the public ear, they are little more than an echo of what a particular audience wants to hear. Somewhere between these two poles, however, there exists a core of important studies whose execution is marked by careful scholarship but whose content is undeniably relevant to the concerns of the citizenry. Stuart A. Wright's *Leaving Cults: The Dynamics of Defection*, stands in the noble tradition of the core.

Such a study entails no small number of risks, of course, especially when the subject matter involves *cults*. Being readable, it is accessible to those who may not fully understand it. Being relevant, it will offend those who disagree with its implications. And being scientific, it may insult the sensibilities of those who assume that scholarship and relevant prose are mutually exclusive items. Nevertheless, *Leaving Cults* takes on those risks and, in so doing, offers its readers a challenge as well: To think carefully and reflectively about one of the more controversial topics of our day. It is a challenge worth taking. Enjoy.

S. D. Gaede
Editor

TABLE OF CONTENTS

LIST OF TABLES

PREFACE

The public furor over cults has waned in recent years. The Bhagwan has been deported, the Children of God have migrated to Third World countries, and one rarely sees Krishna devotees or Moonies selling flowers and distributing literature in the airports or on street corners anymore. Can we thus conclude that religious cult movements are fading and will soon disappear in the near future? Not hardly. If studies are correct, the historical process of secularization in modern societies will continue to give rise to cult formation (Stark and Bainbridge, 1985; Wilson, 1976). Moreover, the decreased visibility of some new religions may be more an indication of changes in organizational goals, strategies, and practices inhering in the process of movement evolution and transformation (Hammond and Bromley, forthcoming; Wright, 1987). Undoubtedly, some movements will die out, others will become socially entrenched, and new ones will be born. Accompanying any future outbreaks of religious enthusiasm and experimentation will be the persistent questions pertaining to conversion, participation, and disengagement. Perhaps the least understood (certainly the least studied) aspect of cult movements is disengagement. Ignoring disengagement has helped to paint an incomplete picture of the cult career. It has impeded an understanding of the degree to which there is an ebb and flow in these movements, and it has given us a distorted image of the individual convert. With this work, I hope to help fill what is in fact a very large void in the literature. My own criteria for judging this effort a success will lie in its ability to generate further dialogue and research on a field of study scarcely touched by social scientists.

In Part One of the book, I attempt to define the problem raised by modern cult movements in an increasingly secular society. I am particularly alarmed by the inclusion of nontraditional but acceptable Christian groups as cults by some psychiatrists and mental health professionals. I endeavor to point out some problems with the widespread use of the term brainwashing and show how the concept is undermined by the form and frequency of voluntary defection. In chapter two, I build a theoretical framework and offer five propositions to test precipitating factors leading to withdrawal. In the next chapter, I discuss some hotly debated issues of cult sponsorship among sociologists of religion and identify my own methods of data collecting and sources of funding.

In Part Two, I am concerned primarily with the causes of disillusionment and patterns of defection. I analyze the theoretical propositions in light of the data and examine the extent of empirical support for each. If defection requires precipitating factors, the process is also helped along by what I call secondary or augmentative factors. These tend to arise as latent goals or interests are marshalled by defectors as added justification or legitimation for quitting. Indeed, the analytical distinction between precipitating and secondary factors point to the fact that defection is a series of withdrawals involving multiple stages of disengagement. As latent goals or interests crystallize, individuals move to the next phase—selecting a mode of exit. Does the individual slip out the back door or does he or she confront the group and negotiate a peaceable leave-taking? Chapter six examines how strategies of departure are planned and establishes linkages between length of membership and modes of exit.

Part Three examines the transition and adjustment phase of defectors after the departure is completed. How is social relocation accomplished? What mechanisms or channels of reintegration are utilized and by whom? Does religion remain an important aspect of defectors' lives, or are they burned out? Equally as important, how do they assess their experiences in retrospect? Do they feel they were manipulated, brainwashed?

Finally, Part Four explores the implications of the findings in terms of public policy. Government regulation and psychiatric intervention often take the form of social weapons to suppress deviance. I suggest this is an unhealthy precedent in a democracy entailing serious civil rights violations camouflaged by medical rhetoric and officious psychiatric diagnoses. Parallel misuses of psychiatry for political ends in the Soviet Union are discussed to illustrate the problem. In a secular society, all nontraditional or enthusiastic religions are implicated, including evangelicalism and fundamentalism, because the revolutionary or charismatic element of religion is not recognized as legitimate by the State or its agents of social control.

Circumstances can create strange bedfellows. The continuing application of brainwashing arguments by mental health professionals has caught the attention of evangelical leaders (Frame, 1983), and forced them to reexamine the merits of these claims, partly because the line between exotic cults and high commitment, sectarian religiosity has become blurred. In effect, some evangelicals now find themselves a target of similar allegations. Is the belief in faith healing cultic? Is speaking in tongues (glossalalia) a sign of fanaticism? Can one believe that God speaks to individuals today and escape the accusation of being a cultist or extremist? What kind of religious expression is socially acceptable and who decides?

Herein lies the paradox of this work. A number of people, including a few ministers and at least one well-known sociologist, have asked me, "Why are you defending cults?" As one with evangelical leanings, I am deeply disturbed by the growth of the Therapeutic State. The emergence of nontraditional or enthusiastic religion is a symptom of problems in the moral fabric of society, perhaps even the failure of mainline churches to meet critical human needs. State repression of unconventional religious expression misses the mark. It fails to take into account many different factors, some of which I have attempted to demonstrate in this monograph. Disengagement provides a comprehensive understanding of participation, and helps to dispel misconceptions of conversion and involvement propagated by the medical model. If anything, it may lead us to ask more penetrating questions about the way in which religious beliefs and expressions change, evolve or dissipate.

ACKNOWLEDGEMENTS

I owe a debt of gratitude to many people who helped make this book possible. The study began as a doctoral dissertation at the University of Connecticut. William M. Newman served as my major advisor and was an inestimable source of encouragement and intellectual stimulation throughout the endeavor. My acquisition of the "sociological imagination" was largely due to our association, culminating (for better or for worse) in that irresistible compulsion to be a professional social scientist, in even the hardest of times. I cannot overstate the importance of his influence on this work nor the value of his friendship. I would also like to acknowledge the contributions of the other members of the thesis committee. William V. D'Antonio was particularly helpful in the formation of ideas regarding marriage and family practices in cult movements. He encouraged me to explore the theoretical linkages between families of converts and disaffiliation. I was fortunate enough to benefit from his expertise before he moved to the busy ASA office in Washington. Myra Marx Ferree supervised the construction of the interview question- naire and help set up the research design. I found her enthusiasm over social research contagious and inspirational. I am also grateful for insightful comments and suggestions she made in chapters five and six.

Several others read all or part of the manuscript at various stages of development. These contributions added immeasurably to the shape and content of the final product. I would be remiss not to mention David Bromley, Helen Ebaugh, William Martin, James Richardson, and Thomas Robbins. I also feel compelled to recognize the contributions made by the post-doctoral fellows group at Yale: Larry Baron, James Parker, Elizabeth Piper, Brent Shea, and Albert Reiss. Their confidence and support helped me to endure yet another round of revisions.

I want to thank Stan Gaede for recognizing the merit of this work and giving me an opportunity to publish in the SSSR Monograph series. He has been courteous, efficient and professional in every phase of our work together. No one could ask more of an editor. I wish to thank Rita Gold, Terrie McGuire, Devra Simpson, and Lynnette Sim- mons for assistance in typing portions of the manuscript. They were more than tolerant of my perfectionism, especially Rita.

I am deeply indebted, of course, to the many people who agreed to be interviewed and take part in this study. This was so much more than simply extracting information. So many people opened up their homes and their personal lives to me in such a way as to allow a strong identification with the feelings, experiences, and beliefs they so vividly described. I found the research experience rich and I have discovered a deep apprecia- tion for the extraordinary people I met during the course of this research.

My extended family has supplied the essential support network I needed to embark on this ambitious project. My parents, Mr. and Mrs. John R. Wright, and my in-laws, Mr. and Mrs. John G. Heard, furnished unending love and confidence throughout, impart- ing to me something that far exceeds the value of the finished manuscript. I also want to acknowledge the support and patience of my wife, Nancy. A close friend once compared writing a book to keeping a mistress. The analogy is appropriate. This mistress was very demanding, imposing frequent marital strains. Yet without Nancy, none of this would have been possible or even desirable. Whatever I have accomplished I share with her. I lovingly dedicate this work to her and to the most important fruit of our labor together—Jenna, Sarah Katherine, and Jared.

Stuart A. Wright

February 15, 1987

PART ONE
DEFINITIONS AND PERSPECTIVES

CHAPTER ONE

BRAINWASHING OR VOLUNTARY PARTICIPATION?

Beginning in the late 1960s and continuing through the decade of the '70s, America witnessed an extraordinary growth of cultic religious movements. While the growth and spread of these movements has subsided in the 1980s, critical scientific, ethical, and legal issues remain unresolved—*issues that will linger long after the groups in question have dissipated or become institutionalized.* For example, some cult movements have been particularly controversial, requiring uncompromising commitment of their members and exhibiting "authoritarian" or "totalistic" beliefs, practices, and lifestyles. Among the most infamous are such groups as the Unification Church ("Moonies"), Scientology, the Children of God/Family of Love, the Hare Krishna, and most recently, the Bhagwan Shree Rajneesh Foundation.[1] These movements have been accused of "brainwashing" their members, and employing techniques of psychological "mind control" and "coercive persuasion" to keep them (Clark, et al., 1981; Conway and Seigelman, 1978; Galper, 1976, E. Levine, 1980; 1982; Patrick, 1976; Shapiro, 1977; Singer, 1979; Verdier, 1977). Members often have been characterized as mindless puppets devoid of rational decision-making capacities and free will. In fact, one legal expert has suggested that cult membership constitutes involuntary servitude and thus should be adjudicated by the courts under laws pertaining to slavery (Delgado, 1979-80). But regardless of how unpalatable one might find these unconventional religious expressions (as most people have), one must ask how accurately has the "brainwashing" metaphor described the overall participation of youth in these groups.[2] More importantly, as we become further removed from the widespread public fears and apprehensions over cult conversion that peaked near the end of the last decade, what kinds of rational and objective assessments can now be made about the so-called brainwashing of converts to unconventional groups, and, in general, what kinds of lessons have been learned? Given the cycle of religious revivals, awakenings, and attendant experimentation (Foster, 1981; McLoughlin, 1978), such "lessons" have far-reaching implications for future generations. An analysis of participation and existing patterns among unconventional religious movements over the past fifteen years can furnish a sensible and informed perspective, both for the present and the future.

Unfortunately, the depiction of religiously committed individuals as brainwashed automatons represents a serious challenge not only to the rights of unconventional religious movements, but ultimately to the viability and freedom of all religious groups. The evidence is compelling. For example, some anti-cultists have stretched brainwashing concepts to describe conservative evangelical Christian groups[3] (Carrol and Bauer,

1979; Conway and Seigelman, 1982; Seigelman and Conway, 1979:68). The term "cult" has been applied indiscriminately to such groups as Catholic Charismatics, Jews for Jesus, Maranantha Campus Ministries, and the Moral Majority. Jews for Jesus, a Hebrew-Christian missionary organization, has been the object of growing anti-cult activity among some traditional Jewish leaders and organizations (Ruby, 1985), despite the lack of empirical evidence for brainwashing (Selengut, 1985). Ted Patrick, the "father" of deprogramming, has asserted that Jerry Falwell has more persons under "mind control" than Reverend Moon and that "Falwell leads the biggest cult in the nation" (Frame, 1983:31). One recent "cult" targeted by deprogrammers appears to be the Assemblies of God denomination. According to one report, an attempted deprogramming in Detroit involved two young women in their early twenties who had joined an affiliate church. Deprogrammers were hired by the mother and stepfather to dissuade the women from their belief in "faith healing" (Frame, 1983:31).

The controversy surrounding brainwashing and interventionist tactics such as "deprogramming" (i.e., the systematic attempt to dissuade individuals—often forcibly—to recant their faith) has centered largely around the issue of voluntary participation and commitment of members. Much has been said and written about deprogrammed ex-members who later claim to have been victims of "mind control" and brainwashing techniques (Conway and Seigelman, 1978; Edwards, 1979; Enroth, 1977; Patrick, 1976; Singer, 1979; Underwood and Underwood, 1979; Verdier, 1977). The rationale of deprogramming rests on the assumption that members of the new religions have been unwittingly "programmed" (Shupe and Bromley, 1980:70-78; Solomon, 1983). Yet, most persons who have joined these movements have left on their own, without the aid of deprogramming. Research suggests that the attrition rate among these new religious groups has been high and that probably only a small percentage of defectors are directly a result of deprogrammings (Shupe and Bromley, 1980:108). In a random sample survey of 200 members of the Unification Church living in centers, Judah (1978:206) found that "fifty-five percent of those surveyed had been in the Church for one year or less." Beckford (1981:14) in a study of the Unification Church in Great Britain, found that "over a two-year period approximately 75 percent of recruits leave the movement." Barker's (1983a) research on "failure rates" within the British Unification Church supports Beckford. She reports that less than 1 in 10 people who attend workshops become core members, and of that group, the majority leave of their own accord within two years of joining. Robbins and Anthony (1980:77) note that "movements such as the Hare Krishna or the Unification Church . . . exhibit a rapid turnover and a high dropout rate." Bromley and Shupe (1979:93) attribute the difficulty of obtaining accurate membership figures for these groups to the "rapid turnover" of participants. In a Montreal study of membership rates in nine new religious movements, Bird and Reimer (1982:5) report that ". . . 75.5 percent of all those who had ever participated in these movements were no longer participants." Consequently, the researchers conclude that the attrition rate among new religious groups in Montreal ". . . is extremely high."[4]

While the evidence for the high dropout rate among the new religions has become incontestable, it has had little impact upon the popular belief that cult members are brainwashed, programmed, psychically coerced or controlled. At least one explanation of such reasoning seems to lie in the larger social and historical context. In the face of encroaching modernity, many people find it difficult to understand intense religious commitment or zeal. For the most part, religion in America has become almost entirely disarmed of its revolutionary or charismatic (Weber, 1963) potential. The customary interaction between religion and culture has been one of "accommodation" and "compromise" (Berger, 1978; Berger and Neuhaus, 1976; Cuddihy, 1975; Hunter, 1983; Luckmann, 1967; Niebuhr, 1929). This is brought sharply into focus when one examines reactions to the resurgence of fundamentalism in recent years, and the ensuing conflicts over abortion, prayer in public schools, the role of women in society, and creationism versus evolutionism. These individuals are seen as "religious fanatics" who stubbornly have spurned modernization processes. The term "fundamentalist" has become an entirely pejorative label. It should not be surprising among observers of the contemporary religious scene to discover fundamentalist and Pentecostal groups lumped in with new religious cults and described as a potential threat to the social equilibrium.

Attributing brainwashing or seduction of converts to unpopular religious groups has been a recurrent theme in history (Cox, 1978; Hargrove, 1980, 1983; Miller, 1983). In the 19th century, anti-Catholic sentiment took a similar form. Cox (1978) has argued that in all societies where novel religious movements have attracted youth, parents and other representatives of the status quo have developed various renditions of the "evil eye" theory, borrowing from contemporary psychological constructs (Hargrove, 1983). "Conversion, in this instance," says Hargrove (1983:303), "is simply a case of induced mental illness." According to Dr. Albert Lubin, chairman of the committee of Psychiatry and Religion for the Group of the Advancement of Psychiatry (GAP),

> When conversion is to a religion that furthers the status quo, society tends to approve of the converts and regard them as normal. When it threatens prevailing beliefs or lifestyles, society often desires to eliminate them either by exile or imprisonment or milder forms of repression and regard them as mentally ill (Ungerleider and Wellisch, 1979:281).

Amidst the continuing popular and professional acceptance of the notion of brainwashing and alleged "destructive cultism" (Clark, et al., 1981; Shapiro, 1977), it is puzzling to find only a modicum of research aimed at studying patterns and processes of disengagement and withdrawal. While numerous studies have suggested that attrition rates are high, we still remain essentially ignorant about how and why they are. Indeed, there has been a much greater expenditure of energy by scholars over the philosophical and ethical concerns than over the pursuit of empirical research. If these issues are ever to be settled, however, it must be because we have increased our knowledge about why people leave and why they stay.

Consequently, the following questions arise: How and why do unconventional religions lose members? What reasons do people give for leaving, and how do they arrive at these decisions? What is the process of voluntary disengagement? What kinds of problems are involved in such a transition? Moreover, how do ex-members, in retrospect, see their experiences? What kinds of attitudes or reactions do they have after they leave? It is essential that we obtain some objective answers to these questions and herein lies the purpose of this study.

Definitions and Directions of the Book

Today one is most likely to hear the word defection used in a political sense, referring perhaps to an individual who left a Soviet bloc country to live in the West. *Webster's Third International Dictionary* (1976) defines defection as "the act of abandoning of a person, cause or doctrine to whom or which one is bound." A political rendering of the term is appropriate, preceding its theological equivalent, apostasy. Apostasy is derived from the classical Greek *apostasia*, meaning political defiance or desertion. In this study, defection will refer to the repudiation of one's identity, belief-system, and social support structure, and the concomitant reconstruction of the same apart from one's previous group or movement. Like the political usage of the term, it is meant to convey a rather serious and fundamental transformation of ideas and behavior. For example, it will involve more comprehensive and deep-seeded changes in one's life than mere "denominational switching."[5] Defection, as employed here, entails a substantial alteration of subjective reality, the abandonment of an identity, friends, and worldview for another way of life.

This book is limited to a study of voluntary or self-initiated withdrawal. Voluntary defection refers to the process of disengagement that occurs without the aid of deprogramming or comparable forms of therapeutic intervention.[6] It is accomplished by the individual without concerted efforts by others to coerce or impel through "techniques" of deconversion. The principal focus of the study is to learn how members of new religions become disaffected and disengage *themselves* from these movements. It is assumed that individuals have the ability to direct and manage their own lives, to make their own decisions, and to pull out of a movement when motivations to continue abate. But how is this accomplished? And what kinds of factors or influences push people to this decision?

Though empirical work on conversion and recruitment to social and religious movements abounds in sociology (see Rambo, 1981 for extensive bibliography), there exists relatively little systematic investigation of defection, deconversion or disaffiliation. The topic of study is not without some research history, but most of it is very recent and related largely to cultic movements. Indeed, this work grows out of a mushrooming interest shared by a number of my colleagues in the sociology of religion. No doubt that in the coming years the volume and depth of research on disaffiliation will rival the research on conversion. It seems quite obvious now that to know why people leave religious groups is just as important as knowing why they join. At present, however, the scale of our knowledge is far from balanced. Only a handful of studies exist to draw upon, though some of them already represent major contributions (Barker, 1983a; Beckford, 1978, 1985; Brinkerhoff and Burke, 1980; Ebaugh, 1977; Mauss, 1969; Skonovd, 1981; Toch, 1965). But more and better research must follow. Many questions remain unanswered and in need of more explicit formulation and explanation.

The findings reported in this volume are taken from a four-year study comparing the reported experiences of current and former members of three new religious movements (Unification Church, Hare Krishna, Children of God/Family of Love). In an effort to advance research and understanding of defection, the study was designed to make two distinctive contributions. First, the data are drawn from a matched sample of defectors and members, the latter serving as a control or comparison group. This point is particularly worth underscoring. A fundamental problem in prior studies is the absence of a comparison group, making explanations of disaffiliation problematic. Methodologically, we cannot say why people leave unless we can say why they stay. In this regard, I offer an empirical, albeit preliminary, test of some theoretical propositions concerning precipitating or triggering factors in the disengagement process. Only a few studies have employed research designs that include comparison groups (see Barker, 1983a; Ebaugh, 1977; Galanter 1983b; Zablocki, 1980) and these are quite diverse and wide-ranging in their objectives. Second, the data gathered from a population of purely voluntary defectors, as opposed to deprogrammed individuals, allows me to focus on a mode of disengagement more commonly experienced among former cult members, and one about which we have less information. It is precisely here I feel that the bulk of future research should be concentrated. While deprogrammings deservedly have gained the ire and attention of social scientists, the mediated influences leading to a deprogrammed individual's choice to leave are not in need of explanation. The role of parents, deprogrammers and/or exit therapists are obvious. What remains to be explained are the influences and events that constitute the majority of cases involving voluntary or self-initiated withdrawal.

Moreover, voluntary leavers disengage themselves from these movements over a much longer period of time than deprogrammed individuals. This makes an impact on both the disengagement sequence and the post-involvement adjustment and transition phase. Decisions are made more slowly, rationales for defection are developed more independently, strategies of leave-taking have to be negotiated and self-implemented, avenues of social reintegration selected, resolution of attitudes toward the group have to be made and assimilated into a new worldview and lifestyle. The manner in which these things are engineered by the voluntary leaver differs significantly from the deprogrammed individual making strict comparisons inappropriate and often misleading. The extent of confusion deriving from such comparisons can be seen in the differing accounts and attitudes regarding the notion of brainwashing discussed toward the end of the book.

I have found the literature on marital separation and divorce helpful in analyzing the gradual disengagement of followers from the group. The comparison between marital love and cultic devotion is most befitting, especially among women who belong to movements with strong charismatic leaders (Jacobs, 1984). Love, sacrifice, and devotion are linked together and expressed in strong emotional attachments, binding members to the group in ways that correspond to the marital commitment. Drawing upon the work of Slater (1963) and Kanter (1972), I argue that the corporate emphasis upon community, harmony, and cohesiveness combined with prohibitions against dyadic exclusivity in certain movements help to create an intense affective catharsis analogous to a group marriage of sorts. In this context, the parallel insights drawn from family researchers studying material separation and divorce are exceptionally illuminating. The dual processes of disengagement resemble each other in many respects, and it is my hope that studies of cult disaffiliation in the future will use the marital disengagement model to guide and inform their analyses. I have invoked this model briefly in an earlier publication (Wright, 1984) but I want to advance the analogy further in this work, if only in a modest way.

But even here, I do not wish to imply that intense cathartic attachments or bonds be interpreted as a form of brainwashing, any more than the solemn bond of matrimony. While the object of commitment may be dissimilar, the sentiments of obligation and connectedness elicited in the individual are not. Actually, the idea is not the least bit revolutionary, since marriage and religious commitment have a long history of metaphoric affinity. The Bible makes numerous references to the church as "the bride of Christ," as well as to the "marriage supper of the Lamb" recorded in the Revelation of John. Similarly, nuns in the Roman Catholic Church have been encouraged for centuries to define and identify themselves as a "spouse of Jesus Christ" (Ebaugh, 1977; San Giovanni, 1978). There is no doubt that commitment levels in Catholic convents are extremely high, but few individuals would advance the notion that they have been manufactured through techniques of psychological mind control.

A sober analysis of disinvolvement from new religions must strive to keep the inquiry within the conceptual framework and language of commitment. In this way, we can view commitment as a continuum, placing different types of relationships or affiliations along a graded scale. The placement of each can be determined by two factors: 1) the motives, goals and willingness of the individual to enjoin himself/herself to the ongoing objectives of the group, and 2) the socialization mechanisms of the organization which are deployed in order to build and maintain the commitment of members. In highly restricted groups like the Unification Church, it then becomes possible to focus on the socialization mechanisms more intently than in less regulated organizations. However, while such mechanisms help to amplify the commitment levels of members, they do not negate the individual's own choices and decisions. To be sure, joining a cultic religious movement involves the act of surrender, but as we shall discover, it is a decision that can be, and often is, revoked.

Finally, it should be made clear that information and research on social disengagement is important in its own right. Disaffiliation is a topic that transcends specific applications such as cult withdrawal. It encompasses a variety of cognitive, emotional, and behavioral forms that pervade our lives. Indeed, life is a perpetual process of entering and exiting social groups and social roles. When we consider what an integral part disengagement plays in human interaction, it is a veritable mystery why the subject hasn't received more attention by scholars. Numerous significant contributions remain to be made. One can only imagine the benefits to be derived from systematic studies of attrition among political parties, businesses, corporations, educational institutions (particularly the teaching profession), churches or denominations, charitable organizations, and so on. For example, the humiliating defeat of the Democratic Party in the 1984 presidential election revealed a mass defection of voters to the Republican ticket. Amidst growing criticism of the Democratic Party's political agenda and the post-election talk of restructuring, a study of defectors' attitudes and convictions would seem most appropriate.

The range and intensity of disengagement varies dramatically. Some types of commitments or affiliations are difficult to relinquish while others are abandoned with relative ease. Cult withdrawal is a type of disengagement that typically is complicated, emotionally disconcerting and often painful. It represents a particular type of disengagement characterized by high levels of difficulty and intensity, largely because prior commitment levels are relatively higher. Therefore, the study addresses only a limited range of disengagement dynamics—those concentrated toward and emanating from the high end of the commitment continuum. I would like to think, however, that the analyses provided here will help shed at least some light on various forms of social disengagement. To make possible some wider applications and generalizations, let me turn to a discussion of theoretical constructs and linkages.

CHAPTER TWO

GAINING AND LOSING COMMITMENT IN NEW RELIGIOUS MOVEMENTS:

SOME THEORETICAL CONSIDERATIONS

A theoretical perspective provides a set of conceptual tools with which to interpret the object of study. By referring to grounded theory in social science, the researcher builds on a foundation of interrelated ideas and concepts that are central to the discipline. Though no single theoretical perspective is comprehensive, each gives a different insight to the problem at hand. The following theoretical purview is particularly useful because it helps to explain how people can inhabit social worlds very different from our own. To understand fully how cults (communities of deviance) can attract members and maintain plausible belief-systems, it becomes necessary to analyze these groups in terms of socialization processes that affect all aspects of human behavior.

The Composition and Decomposition of Social Reality

The theoretical framework of this study is developed from the literature on socialization, particularly as it is understood from a "social construction of reality" perspective (Berger and Luckmann, 1966). Socialization theory tries to explain attitudes and behavior in terms of socio-psychological processes that occur between the individual and society. Ideas, attitudes, actions, indeed the personality of individuals, are formed in an ongoing, dialectical exchange of the ego and the social group. Thus, to understand the values and beliefs of the individual, it is essential to know with which social groups the individual associates and identifies. Embedded in this theory is the idea that subjective reality is pliant and shaped by one's significant social relationships. At the risk of oversimplification, it may be said that one's definition of reality (i.e., worldview) is, to a large extent, a product of one's interaction and identification with a group (plausibility structure). In this context, defection then may be seen as a type of *desocialization*[1] process whereby one loses identification with a social group(s). It involves the transformation of identity, social relations, and worldview. From this perspective I hope to show that joining and leaving a new religious movement is a type of social psychological transition that can be distinguished from other types of major life-changes or transitions (e.g., divorce, retirement) only by degree. Let us now take a closer look at these ideas as they provide a framework for understanding religious socialization and commitment.

Subjective reality is fluid, dynamic, and malleable. Individuals change their views and attitudes as they grow older, are exposed to new ideas, affiliate with different people, join new social groups, change jobs, or experience geographical or social class mobility. Subjective reality is particularly influenced by one's social relationships because it is largely informed by collective definitions and expectations of behavior. As our associations with different collectivities change, individuals seek stable environments wherein one finds people with similar lifestyles, attitudes, and values. These environments provide individuals with a sense of identity, meaning, and camaraderie. Berger and Luckmann (1966:154) refer to such environments as "plausibility structures." A plausibility structure refers to "the specific social base and social processes required for (the) maintenance" of social reality. An individual maintains an identity as a scholar, a Marxist, or an artist essentially because he or she is located within such a plausibility structure that affirms that identity. Concomitantly, one can maintain a religious faith more easily if one preserves his or her significant relationships within the religious community. Indeed, the disruption of social contact threatens the viability of one's plausibility structure (Berger and Luckmann, 1966:155).

Plausibility structures also serve as a social base by which suspension of doubts is effectively accomplished. Contradictory or adverse evaluations are likely to be dismissed by group personnel. Specific sanctions against invalid expressions or doubts may be invoked by other group members, or they may be internalized by the individual in the form of self-criticism and attributed to personal shortcomings, weaknesses, or lack of faith (Mead, 1934:255). Socially shared beliefs are less vulnerable to disconfirming evidence when firmly grounded in a strong plausibility structure, even when such evidence seems obvious (Festinger, et al., 1964).

Like other social groups, the new religions are collectivities that create and maintain social realities through plausibility structures. Regardless of how bizarre or unorthodox these collectivities may appear to outsiders, the necessary apparatus for sustaining beliefs and commitment among members continues to operate effectively in the context of strong plausibility structures. These "deviant" social environments, however, are not easily developed or maintained. Cults or new religions must implement processes that help build, strengthen, and sustain the plausibility structures that make commitment both possible and desirable. Such processes involve socialization procedures that augment the legitimacy of groups beliefs and practices while diminishing the viability of competing social realities. The tactic of minimizing or eliminating rival beliefs and perspectives is referred to by Berger and Luckmann (1966:155) as "nihilation." Nihilation is imperative in controlling the problem of "backsliding" because it continually reduces the importance of alternative choices or commitments. Nihilation is also an important part of the conversion process.

> The nihilating side of the conceptual machinery is particularly important in view of the dismantling problem that must be solved. The old reality, as well as the collectivities and significant others that previously mediated it to the individual must be reinterpreted "within" the legitimating apparatus of the new reality. This reinterpretation brings about a rupture in the subjective biography of the individual in terms of "B.C." and "A.D.," "pre-Damascus" and "post-Damascus." . . . Pre-alternation biography is typically nihilated *in toto* by subsuming it under a negative category occupying a strategic position in the new legitimating apparatus: "When I was still living a life of sin," "When I was still caught up in bourgeois consciousness," "When I was still motivated by these unconscious neurotic needs." The biographical rupture is thus identified with a cognitive separation of darkness and light (Berger and Luckmann, 1966:159-160).

Nihilation is a common strategy employed by religious movements to detach individuals from their previous beliefs and ties. It offers an interpretive framework from which to re-evaluate the "old" way of thinking and acting. Members may be encouraged to offer similar "testimonies" of the darkness-to-light transition thus validating collective perceptions and beliefs. Similarly, groups may point to situations or events in the larger social world that "confirm" the "outer darkness" that pervades culture.

To complement nihilation, socialization procedures are implemented to enhance the value of belonging to the group. The new religions typically make claims to possessing the "key" to unique personal or social transformations which promise a better life or a new social order. Group leaders are likely to stress the exclusive moral status of the movement and the spiritual rewards that accrue from participation. Ideals of spiritual unity, brotherhood, and community are emphasized, as is their translation into acts of self-sacrifice for the good of the group.

When socialization processes initiated by the group are subjectively apprehended by the individual as consonant with his or her own beliefs or perspective, the result is commitment. Commitment arises when group socialization processes and individual ideas and interests merge. Kanter (1972:66) argues that, "Commitment arises as a consideration at the intersection between the organizational (behavioral) requisites of groups and the personal (mental) orientations and preferences of their members." Commitment to a group and adoption of its plausibility structure is a give-and-take process. One submits to its regulations and controls and, in turn, receives the benefits of what the group has to offer both emotionally and cognitively. The group links personal orientations to group perspectives and goals through socialization processes or mechanisms. The effective use of socializing mechanisms increases the likelihood that commitment will be upheld.

To commit oneself to a religious world is to abide by and accept the socialization processes that stabilize its plausibility. It is to internalize the collective definitions and expectations of appropriate behavior and practice, and observe them as one's own. Commitment is sustained through socialization processes that protect that which is valued by the collective. It requires sacrifice, investment, and the surrendering of one's personal time, energy, and lifestyle. At the same time it provides meaning, purpose, and identity. Commitment, of course, is a matter of degree; one's identification with and acceptance of group expectations can vary considerably. Thus, the greater the conformity to and acceptance of group socialization, the greater the level of commitment.

The maintenance of belief and commitment is a process that must be continually renewed and strengthened. Individually, members must continue to make social and psychological investments in the group so that their commitment will be perceived as meaningful and worthwhile. One's time, energy, or money is just such an investment that affirms devotion and self-sacrifice. When sacrifices are made by members, their motivation to remain as followers increases. According to Kanter (1972:76), this "operates on the basis of a simple principle from cognitive consistency theories: the more it 'costs' a person to do something, the more 'valuable' he will consider it, in order to justify the psychic 'expense' and remain internally consistent."

In many religions, sacrifice has been conceptualized as an act of consecration, bringing one closer to and making one more worthy of the deity. A vow of poverty, for example, may aid commitment. In the eyes of the group and in the mind of the individual, sacrifice for a cause makes it sacred and inviolable. It also represents a gesture of trust in the group, indicating how important membership is (Kanter, 1972:76-77).

Membership in a religious group involves not only sacrificing extraneous interests, at times, but also postponing immediate gratifications (Wilson, 1973:301). When individuals are willing to give their time and resources to a cause, they commit themselves to a consistent course of action.

From an organizational standpoint, religious movements that successfully persuade members to make sacrifices for the benefit of the group and its mission are more likely to have a higher level of commitment among their members (Kanter, 1972:76-80; Wilson, 1973:301-303). "Commitment," says Wilson (1973:302-3), "demands the surrender of self; individual claims to time, energy, and resources are sacrificed for the general good. . . . The greater the suppression of personal proclivities, the greater the degree of commitment."

From the individual standpoint, the would-be follower recognizes that he or she cannot accomplish significant social change alone. The individual needs the group. Each individual has to make sacrifices in order to make an impact. Group objectives are more easily realized when members are willing to surrender personal interests and considerations to the movement. In addition, the individual finds comfort and emotional support in the company of like-minded believers. By becoming part of the group, the individual gains strong social ties, relatedness, and a sense of belonging. Each member feels encouraged and inspired by a common sharing of ideals and purposes.

Commitment is strengthened considerably as individuals adopt, either partially or totally, the group's plausibility structure, which acts to support and maintain socially shared definitions about the world. But commitment is more than an initial decision or conversion to a perspective. It is an ongoing process that is developed and strengthened through interaction, identification, and cooperation with other committed followers. According to Berger and Luckmann, the problem of commitment lies not in achieving conversion but in maintaining identity and conviction after the initial experience.

> To have a conversion experience is nothing much. The real thing is to keep on taking it seriously; to retain a sense of its plausibility. *This* is where the religious community comes in, it provides the indispensible plausibility structure for the new reality. In other words, Saul may have become Paul in the solitude of religious ecstasy, but he could *remain* Paul only in the context of the Christian community that recognized him as such and confirmed the "new being" in which he now located this identity. . . . Religion requires a religious community, and to live in a religious world requires affiliation with that community (1966:158).

Commitment to a religious group is an agreement to abide by and accept the socialization processes that stabilize its plausibility. This involves adopting as one's own the collective guidelines for appropriate behavior. Individuals submerge themselves in the group to further that which is personally and collectively valued.

New Religions as Social Movements

The new religions selected for this study (Unification Church, Hare Krishna, Children of God) are also social movements that seek to change society. A social movement may be defined as an organized group whose primary goal is to create or resist change by noninstitutionalized means (Wilson, 1973:8). According to one theory, social movements emerge out of "structural strains" within the social system (Smelser, 1962). The "institutionalization of a system creates the possibility that 'antisystems' or groups with negative orientation towards its premises will develop within it" (Eisenstadt, 1964:247). Thus, social movements represent organized efforts at redressing grievances or proposing new solutions to perceived problems or inadequacies within the system. Generally excluded from the normal institutional channels of change, social movements arise to challenge the existing social order and to declare alternatives to achieve commonly valued objectives. They reflect the way in which the old social order has become ineffective, irrelevant, or unresponsive to the needs of a particular segment of the population.

Social movements are also "social inventions" (Coleman, 1970) that provide ways of coping with social stress. Such inventions frequently involve new social microcosms reflecting the new order (Robbins, 1981:215). For example, millenarian movements and utopian communal experiments represent social inventions of this nature (Foster, 1981; Kanter, 1972; Kephart, 1982). These movements organize efforts and develop resources for acting out the changes they hope to implement in society.

Social movements supply the articulated rationale and context for personal and social transformation. "They function to move people beyond their mundane selves to acts of bravery, savagery, and selfless charity. Animated by the injustices, sufferings, and anxieties they see around them, men and women reach beyond the customary resources of the social order to launch their own crusade against the evils of society" (Wilson, 1973:5). In the company of other participants or reformers, individuals transcend their own limitations to become new men and women and set in motion the possibility of a new social form.

Much of the recent work on social movements revolves around the "resource mobilization" perspective, which tends to stress the *rationality* of both individual participation and organizational strategies (Gamson, 1975; McCarthy and Zald, 1977; Tilly, 1978). This approach relies more on political, economic, and social organizational theories than upon the social psychology of collective behavior (Zald and McCarthy, 1979:2). Specifically, the contribution of the resource mobilization perspective has been to highlight the logic of movement organization strategies and actions, as opposed to the idea that social movements are products of collective impulse, and to show how they derive from conscious and deliberate planning. The contribution made by this approach is invaluable to the study of social movements. However, it has been argued that the resource mobilization approach understates the importance of the social psychological and ideological components of social movements (Ferree and Miller, 1985). While serving as a corrective to earlier excesses in the "hearts and minds" approach, the resource mobilization perspective now may be accused of the same immoderation because of its one-sided emphasis on organizational factors and rational self-interest. Marx (1979) has addressed this issue and calls for a balance in theoretical perspective.

A major future challenge for analysts of social movements lies in bringing together the resource mobilization perspective with its emphasis on organizational variables and rational self-interest, with the collective behavior perspective with its emphasis on emotion, expression, symbols, and fluid nature of mass involvement (1979:123).

Marx's challenge serves as a major goal in my own analysis. The two different perspectives described above are seen as essentially complementary. Social organizations are not always as rational and deliberate as they would like to believe. Such characteristics may even be a hindrance to the efficiency of the organization (Blau, 1963). Also, the success of a movement sometimes may depend more upon the charismatic qualities of a leader than on conscious planning and organization of resources. The Father Divine movement is one such example (Cantril, 1963:132-33). On the other hand, participation in unorthodox religious movements may be interpreted as perfectly logical, or justified in terms of self-interest (Snow and Machelek, 1982). Some new religious movements find no contradiction in developing highly organized fundraising operations to promote "spiritual" causes (Bromley and Shupe, 1980). In short, there is a considerable overlapping of organizational and social psychological variables, and any serious study of social movements must take both into account.

In a classic work on collective behavior, Smelser (1962) suggests that there are basically two types of social movements: 1) norm-oriented, and 2) value-oriented. The first refers to efforts by collectivities to impose limited change of specific norms, while the second refers to collective attempts to "restore, protect, modify, or create values in the name of a generalized belief." Value-oriented movements deal with the most fundamental aspects of society and culture in order to resist or induce change. More recently, Bromley and Shupe (1979) have built upon Smelser's earlier work, employing a resource mobilization perspective in analyzing the Unification Church. They use the term "world-transforming movement" to refer to the same three groups selected for this study (Shupe and Bromley, 1979:326). Bromley and Shupe (1979:22) add the dimension of "amount" of change to Smelser's typology, using Aberle's (1966) dichotomy of "partial" and "total" change. World-transforming movements are essentially aimed at bringing about permanent, widespread moral and institutional change through peaceful means. These movements seek sweeping alterations in contemporary society that involve the transition to a new age or new social order. World-transforming movements reject many dominant cultural values, traditions, beliefs, and institutions. They strive to "create a social order which is incompatible with the established order" (Shupe and Bromley, 1980:236).[2] The following paragraphs identify the essential characteristics of world-transforming movements.

In terms of ideology, world-transforming movements predict total and imminent change while placing themselves within an interpretation of history that affirms the necessity and inevitability of that change. The source of current social ills is typically located in some intractable human dilemma that has persisted throughout history and culminated in the present world. World-transforming movements believe that the unprecedented opportunity for resolution of the problem must be seized because sudden and cataclysmic change is virtually around the corner. The ideology also identifies and outlines the unique historical role of the movement in facilitating this transformation (Bromley and Shupe, 1979:27).

World-transforming movements typically possess charismatic leadership. The founder-leader is the dominant charismatic authority in the early stages of the movement (e.g., Reverend Moon, Moses David Berg, A. C. Bhaktivedanta). The leadership structure of the movement is pyramidal. Secondary leaders are designated by the founder-leader and serve as devoted disciples. The secondary leaders themselves often compete for favor with the charismatic leader and occupy a status that is "clearly separate from the mass of movement members" (Bromley and Shupe, 1979:28).

Though world-transforming movements seek rapid and total change, they initially have only a small number of members. This has at least two implications for mobilization and growth if these groups are to achieve their goals. First, commitment must be *total* because the movement requires maximum effort from the few members they claim in order to realize the new social order. Second, recruitment must be aggressive and vigorous in order to win new recruits and warn society of the impending transformation. Therefore, these groups must rely on rapid and effective tactics of recruitment, socialization, and commitment-building. Because of the urgency with which they envision their mission and the limited control of resources they possess, world-transforming movements exercise little selectivity in recruiting and tend to rely more on intensive socialization processes to secure commitment.

World-transforming movements usually *must rely on intensive socialization of new recruits due to low selectivity.* Such movements often lack a clear conception of the type of individual who can be attracted to the movement and have a low success rate; as a result they are forced to rely on self-selection for new members. *Intensive socialization practices both substitute for selectivity in recruitment and help to foster and sustain a high level of commitment* (Bromley and Shupe, 1979:28).

In terms of structural organization, world-transforming movements are highly regulated and supervised. Ideally, regulation and coordination can be enhanced within communally based structures—a feature shared by the core memberships of the three movements studied here. In the context of a communal organization, a strong plausibility structure acts to safeguard members against numerous countervailing forces in the larger society. World-transforming movements face the social reproach and cognitive hegemony of the surrounding society which may have the effect of undermining commitment. But within the support network of a highly structured communal organization, these disruptive forces are greatly diminished. The communal lifestyle helps to erect a more durable plausibility structure that is less likely to be penetrated and destroyed.

This type of organizational structure also increases the ability of the group to conduct intensive socialization effectively. For example, routine schedules are designed so that members will spend many hours a day in collective activities such as lectures, training sessions, rituals, and ceremonies. Communal living arrangements encourage openness and unity with the group while discouraging individualistic actions and pursuits. Members are expected to minimize outside ties with families and friends in order to devote full time and energies to the movement. They are also encouraged to donate their worldly possessions to the movement, to change their behavior, their dress, and even their names. Moreover, members are expected to abide by unconventional sexual practices and alternative marriage and family lifestyles (celibacy, arranged marriages, sexual pluralism).

These conditions are absolutely crucial to the success of world-transforming movements from both an organizational and social psychological standpoint. Kanter (1972) has shown that the requisites just described act as commitment-building mechanisms that strengthen corporate identity, cohesion, and social control. She argues that intensive socialization procedures increase the survival ability of social or religious movements. Other research supports this contention. Zald and Ash (1966:332) argue that movement organizations with easy conditions of membership are likely to fade away faster than ones with rigorous conditions. Richardson, *et al.*, (1979:332) state that "groups which early on develop rigorous resocialization procedures have shown more survival ability."

Through specific socialization and commitment-building processes, organizational requisites come to be interpreted by committed members as personal imperatives. The primary task of socializing new members lies in leading them to a point at which personal identity and subjective reality come to be seen as coextensive with the group. Commitment, says Kanter (1968:499), refers to the "willingness of social actors to give their energy and loyalty to social systems, the attachment of personality systems to social relations which are seen as self-expressive." When socializing mechanisms are effective, even arduous and menial tasks are defined as having a high degree of importance to the individual's moral and spiritual state. Acts of self-sacrifice are interpreted as "building-blocks" of faith, and adherence to restrictive or rigid beliefs become personal challenges of devotion and loyalty.

Some Theoretical Propositions

The process of commitment, however, is *always* subject to interruption whereby prior socialization can be impaired and leaving becomes an alternative. Socialization mechanisms employed by world-transforming movements simply try to reduce the likelihood of interruptions occurring. When interruptions occur, the processes that sustain beliefs and commitment lose their binding force upon the individual. Interruptions come in the form of invalidating experiences or perceptions and initiate disengagement. They represent precipitating factors or influences that generate dissonance and disaffection leading to withdrawal. Of course, defection, like commitment, is a *process*. No claim is made here that the factors identified in the following propositions constitute the single solitary causes of defection. However, defection does not occur in a vacuum. Certain experiences or events are fundamentally more important in creating dissonance and disconfirmation, in engendering defection. What is set forth here are primary factors and influences that set into motion the defection process.

PROPOSITION ONE: *The less the degree to which the world-transforming movement effectively provides insulation from the larger society, the greater the likelihood of defection.* Insulation refers to the extent to which social interaction and communication with the larger culture is reduced and regulated. Thus, prescribed modes of interaction with outsiders are typically restricted to recruitment, fundraising, or some other activity regarded as beneficial to the movement. Insulation is important for all members of a movement operating in a hostile environment wherein the movement's right to exist is constantly being challenged. Turner and Killian (1957:481) argue that insulating boundaries are crucial to social movements because they keep members away from antagonistic assessments of the organization. Robertson (1967:132) attributes the lack of success among millenarian movements in the West to their failure to effectively insulate themselves. Essentially, all social movements face the need to protect themselves from others who oppose them (Wilson, 1973:317).

Communal organization plays an important role in creating and sustaining insulation.[3] Dependence upon society is minimal since members' daily needs are generally met within the group. Such detachment and segregation enhance movement definitions of an externally corrupt world and help to promote internal attitudes of unity and solidarity in the context of a regulated community. "Perhaps most important," state Shupe and Bromley (1980:236), "the communal group constitutes an actualized microcosm of the new social order which movement members envision and hence sustains the intense commitment and involvement requisite for communal organization."

Insulation helps to filter negative information and avert conditions heightening vulnerability. When counterpropaganda has been heard, the group may help to neutralize doubts. Skonovd (1981:37) observes that "the power of the affective social environment to dispel doubts arising from interactions outside the collectivity is virtually limitless." However, when insulating boundaries are disrupted, weakened, or dissolved, commitment is more likely to be damaged by disconfirming evidence and the likelihood of defection increases.

PROPOSITION TWO: *The less the degree to which the world-transforming movement effectively regulates two-person intimacy, the greater the likelihood of defection.* One possible source of defection arises when one partner of a dyad wishes to leave and attempts to persuade the other to defect also. Kanter (1972:86) argues that "two-person intimacy poses a threat to group cohesiveness unless it is somehow controlled or regulated. [Thus] . . . an intense, private two-person relationship . . . is the sort of unit that can potentially withdraw from involvement with the group." Exclusive two-person bonds create rival interests and divert emotional energies from the movement (Slater, 1963). Where these dyadic bonds are not subordinated adequately to the group, disengagement by one partner will more likely have a greater impact upon the other.

World-transforming movements attempt to discourage and regulate exclusive attachments of couples through such practices as celibacy, arranged marriages, and sexual pluralism. These practices require that members relinquish personal control over sexual intimacy to the group, thereby eliminating competition for primary loyalties and emotional attachments. Celibacy and arranged marriages are perhaps the most obvious forms of social control. Both are practiced by the Hare Krishna and the Unification Church. Sexual pluralism or group marriage is a less obvious form of social control but has the same function of securing primary loyalties by diffusing emotional bonds throughout the group (Kanter, 1972; Slater, 1963:349). Sexual pluralism, a practice of the Children of God/Family of Love (Pritchett, 1985; Richardson and Davis, 1983; Wallis, 1976, 1978, 1979), has the effect of creating group cohesiveness by eliminating "private twosomes" when they compete with commitment to the movement. Moses David, the charismatic leader of the Children of God, makes this point explicit in a letter to his followers.

THE FAMILY MARRIAGE, THE SPIRITUAL REALITY BEHIND SO-CALLED GROUP MARRIAGE, IS THAT OF PUTTING THE LARGER FAMILY FIRST, even above the last remaining vestige of private property, your husband, or your wife! . . .
. . . WHAT THE WORLD THINKS ARE OUR WEAKNESSES ARE ACTUALLY OUR STRENGTHS. We do not minimize the marriage ties, as such. We just consider our ties to the Lord and the larger Family greater and more important. And when the private marriage ties interfere with Our Family and God ties, they can be readily abandoned for the glory of God and the good of the Family! We are not forsaking the marital unit.—We are adopting a greater and more important and far larger concept of marriage: The totality of the Bride and her marriage to the Bridegroom is the Family (Berg, 1976:1367).

Since the mid-'70s sexual pluralism in the Children of God movement increasingly has taken the forms of sexual recruitment practices (flirty fishing or "FFing") and most recently, triadic relations, typically polygynous in form (Berg, 1981).

When world-transforming movements do not effectively regulate private two-person bonds and redirect commitment to the larger "family," they face the greater possibility that when one partner wants to leave, he or she will convince the other to defect as well. Therefore, the movement must exercise control over sexual intimacy in order to secure total commitment and deter attrition by couples.

PROPOSITION THREE: *The less the degree to which members of the world-transforming movement perceive the regulation of their time, lifestyle, labor, and sexual conduct as an urgent necessity, the greater the likelihood of defection.* Because the new age or new social order is believed to be imminent, *urgency* plays a crucial role in providing justification for extreme sacrifices made by members. Incentives for such extreme sacrifices are closely tied to the urgency or exigency with which these groups envision their mission. Individuals usually join these movements with very high expectations of immediate and sweeping success. However, when this success is not realized, a diminished sense of urgency may set in bringing disappointment, disillusionment, and frustration, and thus heightening the probability of defection.

To illustrate the underlying importance of urgency to movements of this nature, I refer again to the writings of Moses David, founder-leader of the Children of God.

WE ARE THE LAST CHURCH! We are God's last hope, the last step in God's progress toward *total freedom* for His Church and the *last chance* to prove that the *ultimate Church* can be trusted with *total freedom* in this *last generation*! . . . EACH AGE OR GENERATION OF THE CHURCH HAS TAKEN ANOTHER STEP TO- WARD SUCH FREEDOM from harsh restrictions of the law to total freedom of *love* through the grace of God; from *material symbolisms* and *mechanized ceremonialism* to *spiritual realities* and *total spiritual liberty*—the spirits of just men are free" (Berg, 1974)!

In the text of the "Mo letter," one may observe that in the first two sentences alone he employs a series of five phrases using the adjective "last": "LAST CHURCH," "last hope," "last step," "last chance," "last generation." The pervasive sense of urgency with which the prophet-leader conveys this key doctrine or belief is clearly evident. Similarly, the Unification Church has stressed the urgency of its mission due to the belief that 1981 was to mark the beginning of the millennium (Bromley and Shupe, 1979:97; Lofland, 1977:281). The Hare Krishna hold the belief that the present materialistic age of Kali-Yuga soon will be interrupted by a ten thousand-year reign of peace referred to as the "Golden Age."[3] This shared sense of urgency is in fact a characteristic of all world-transforming movements. "All such movements," Bromley and Shupe (1979:52) state, "are committed to at least forewarning populaces of the impending transformation."

However, if the perceived contribution or value of personal sacrifices come to be seen as unwarranted in a less-than-urgent time frame, the likelihood of defection increases. Members must be continually reassured that there is a compelling need to make extensive personal sacrifices.

PROPOSITION FOUR: *The less the degree to which members of the world-transforming movement perceive the organization as fulfilling the affective needs of a primary or quasi-primary group, the greater the likelihood of defection.* Sociologists argue that some new religions have served the function of primary or quasi-primary groups which offer strong affective environments within communal settings. These movements are attractive to young persons because they offer a way of "recapturing and returning ultimate control over affective legitimacy to groups . . . which resemble extended families" (Robbins and Anthony, 1980:81). Some claim the disintegration of the nuclear family forces youth to fulfill affective needs in cults which act as "surrogate families" (Doress and Porter, 1981:279). Not surprisingly, these movements frequently employ familial terms such as "spiritual parents," "Father," "Mother," "True Parents," "perfect family," "unified family," "brother," "sister," etc., to define their own interactional relations and roles. They also seek to realize goals of unity, love, spiritual harmony, and brotherhood. Joining these movements may be an attempt by some youth to secure "loving interpersonal relations as well as a pure physical and moral environment—free of the violence, promiscuity, drug abuse, and moral ambiguity that pervade the 'outer darkness' of society" (Robbins and Anthony, 1981:27). However, when these primary relationships come to be seen as impersonal, indifferent, or unloving, the likelihood of defection increases.

World-transforming movements typically claim to practice unparalleled levels of love and spiritual harmony within the communal organization. But interpersonal affectivity may be lost in the more mundane demands of meeting movement goals and objectives. For example, imposed constraints or various social control mechanisms may override ideals of love, or unanticipated interaction may reflect unloving or uncaring attitudes leading to disaffection. When such incidents occur, the likelihood of defection increases.

PROPOSITION FIVE: *The less the degree to which members perceive the leadership of the world-transforming movement as "exemplary," the greater the likelihood of defection.* Weber (1963:55) describes the role of an "exemplary" leader or prophet as one who directs others down the same path of salvation he himself traveled. The concept of exemplary leadership is modified and extended here to include actions by all leaders (the prophet-leader and secondary leaders) that are perceived as ethically or morally consistent with the ideals and goals of the movement. The legitimacy of the movement leadership may be undermined if there are behavioral inconsistencies or contradictions. Research suggests that American converts have been motivated to join these movements out of disillusionment with the moral ambiguities found in dominant cultural institutions and values (Bellah, 1976; Robbins and Anthony, 1980). Therefore, it would be reasonable to assume that observed inconsistencies between espoused ideals and actual practices by movement leaders would produce among some converts the same disillusionment that motivated them to reject mainstream culture initially.

Commitment to a world-transforming movement involves a high degree of "trust" invested by members in the leadership (Wilson, 1973:204). These leaders are believed to be the spokespersons of great moral and spiritual truths; they are the entrusted officials of the new social order. Movement leaders are thus deemed worthy of members' devotion and loyalty. If, however, the relationship of trust is violated by actions that are seen as contradictory or morally inconsistent, dissonance is likely to be created. When perceptions or experiences of this nature arise so that the leadership is no longer seen as "exemplary," the likelihood of defection increases.

The five propositions I have identified on the preceding pages target the initial stage of defection. I intend to discuss and analyze these in much greater detail in chapter four, followed by a delineation of progressive levels of withdrawal in the subsequent chapters. But before proceeding further, it may be helpful to provide a description of the methods and sample used in this study.

CHAPTER THREE
STAYERS AND LEAVERS: METHODOLOGICAL CONSIDERATIONS

It is a common practice among writers and publishers of scholarly books to relegate technical methodological discussions to appendices for the sake of the reader. And in the majority of cases I welcome de-methodologized versions of sociological literature. But rarely does the methodology become a central issue in a controversy the way it has in the study of cults. The very methods of research, interpretations of findings, and sources of funding in cult studies have prompted major debates and controversies in and among themselves (Barker, 1983b; Beckford, 1978, 1983; Horowitz, 1978, 1983; Kilbourne, 1983; Robbins, 1983, 1984, 1985a; Robertson, 1985; Wallis, 1983; Wilson, 1983; Wright, 1984). For example, some scholars have challenged the scientific objectivity of research where there appears to be direct or indirect forms of sponsorship by the religious organizations in question. In this regard, Horowitz (1983:179) asks, ". . . what compels otherwise highly refined scientific and social scientific imaginations to become representative spokepersons, even apologists for . . . theological special interests?" Allegations of indirect forms of sponsorship have been made in reference to honoraria and expense-paid trips to cult-sponsored conferences. Horowitz claims such activities imply covert alliances and impugn the integrity of academic scholarship. Bryan Wilson (1983) and others have denied co-optation and defended their research pointing to accepted standards of sympathetic detachment and disinterested involvement. But Beckford (1983) has illustrated the complexity of the problem citing an incident in which a representative of the Unification Church attempted to influence the findings of his study.

On the other side, some recent research has uncovered serious technical and methodological flaws in key anticult studies, severely discrediting their results (Kilbourne, 1983; Wright, 1984). Kilbourne conducted a rigorous secondary analysis of the data collected by Conway and Seigelman (1978) in order to evaluate the statistical validity of proposed relationships between "information disease" and certain types of cult activity. Contrary to conclusions by the original authors, he found that 1) average time in the group and 2) average hours per day in ritual process did *not* correlate significantly with either long-term mental and emotional effects or average rehabilitation time (Kilbourne, 1983:382).[1] Wright (1984) has challenged the findings of studies which rely on responses of deprogrammed ex-members to adduce evidence for brainwashing, demonstrating marked differences in accounts between deprogrammed and voluntary leavers.

Furthermore, clinical research by psychiatrists and mental health professionals has been accused of psychological reductionism vis-à-vis a "medicalization of deviance" model (Hargrove, 1980; Robbins, 1979, 1981; Robbins and Anthony, 1982). Some observers persist in analyzing cult involvement and commitment in terms of induced psychological deprivation and mind control (Clark, *et al.*, 1981; Galper, 1976, 1982; Shapiro, 1977; Verdier, 1977). Debates continue to rage, leading one sociologist to lament that the basic argument over brainwashing ". . . is largely definitional and not susceptible to empirical resolution" (Robbins, 1984:248). However, such conclusions may prove to be a bit premature.

In light of the concerns recounted above, I feel it is imperative to include an abridged description of the data collection methods and a profile of the sample which was used. The discussion in this chapter is divided into three sections. The first section deals briefly with a delineation of data gathering procedures. The second section examines sample characteristics. The third section identifies some issues involved in using subjective accounts as empirical data and explains how these were handled. While some basic techniques and features require explanation, I do not intend to overburden the reader here. Additional information and details are supplied in appendix A.

How the Data Were Collected

It should be clarified at the outset that the study was not sponsored in any way either by anticult organizations or by the religious organizations which are the focus of this research. Funding for the study was provided through grants by the National Science Foundation and National Institutes for Mental Health.[2]

The three new religious movements selected for this study were the Children of God, the Hare Krishna, and the Unification Church ("Moonies"). My reasons for choosing these three particular groups were simple. They are among the most controversial of the new religions (Robbins and Anthony, 1980a) and thus represent the extreme cases, in which defection is a near-total transformation of identity, lifestyle, and perspective. Logically, then, we should be able to say that if the processes involved in the extreme cases are clarified, those of less extreme cases will be understood more easily.

Because of the special problem posed by locating defectors from these groups, it was decided that the data could best be obtained by a snowball sampling technique. In this kind of technique, "the researcher builds up a sample of a special population by asking initial informants to supply names of other potential sample members" (Smith, 1975:118). The snowball method yields a self-selected, purposive sample, and is best suited for targeting a relatively diffuse and inaccessible population (see Babbie, 1975:203; Eckhardt and Ermann, 1977:253). "Snowball techniques are most useful when there is a need to identify a previously unknown population" (Eckhardt and Ermann, 1977:253). By asking respondents to identify other potential sample members, it becomes possible to link members of an unknown population to each other, either directly or indirectly. The obvious benefit of this method is that it enables one to uncover members of a target population that are not tied together in any type of formal organization.[3] They are virtually invisible and inaccessible except through informal friendship networks.

Data for the project were gathered from ninety in-depth interviews. The interviews were based on structured questionnaires and were divided evenly between defectors (N = 45) and a comparison group of current members (N = 45). The sample was further subdivided so that defectors and members of each movement were equally represented (see Table 3.1). A battery of closed and open-ended questions were used to gather a wide range of information about why individuals chose to leave, or as in the case of current members, not to leave.

Table 3.1. MEMBERS AND DEFECTORS BY RELIGIOUS GROUP

	Defectors	Members	Total
Children of God	15	15	30
Hare Krishna	15	15	30
Unification Church	15	15	30
	45	45	N = 90

The interviews were conducted between June 1979 and December 1980. Initial respondents were solicited primarily through printed posters and newspaper ads on several major campuses in the Northeast. The posters requested the aid of former members of the three religious movements to relate personal experiences of their involvement, and a telephone number was given with which to make contact. Similarly, ads were placed in campus newspapers using the identical wording found on the posters. Those responding to the solicitations were interviewed and in turn asked to identify other potential respondents, and so on. While the names and whereabouts of previously known friends or fellow devotees who defected often amounted to just fragments of information, this still proved to be the most effective method of locating ex-members. However, I also turned to halfway houses, religious agencies, and anticult organizations for help in identifying defectors as well (see appendix A).

As I observed in the first chapter, we cannot really explain why people leave unless we can show why they stay. Therefore, it was determined that the best way to isolate critical or explanatory factors in disaffiliation would be to compare the responses of leavers to a matched sample of stayers. The use of a comparison group makes it possible to assess whether or not factors that might help explain the phenomenon in question are operating only among the target group. For example, in a study of conversion among students to Catholic Pentecostalism, Heirich (1977) found that conventional explanations that pointed to prior stress were seemingly supported in the absence of a comparison group. However, when the comparison group of non-converts was examined, it was found that a comparably high number of persons in the general population also reported prior stress situations, thus disconfirming the stress theory of conversion (Heirich, 1977:664-65).

Interviews with current members were obtained with the permission of local organizational authorities of each group. The selection process involved two methods. Sixty-nine percent of the control sample came from four local organizational centers, whose membership was sufficiently small to interview all full-time participants. The remaining members were sampled in two large, centralized headquarters in New York and Boston. The members interviewed there were those available by virtue of assigned in-house duties (designated on a rotating basis). Generally, it was found that organizations were reasonably cooperative in these efforts. Church officials were simply told that the research was designed to augment sociological knowledge about their respective groups and no specific aims of the study were discussed or divulged. Movement authorities in no way sought to influence the content of the interview and to the best of my knowledge made no attempt to influence the response of the participants. Interviews were conducted in complete privacy and typically lasted between one and two hours. Finally, no claim for representativeness can be made here. While the matched samples are quite similar with regard to social characteristics, the techniques employed do not provide random selections from the populations of leavers and stayers. Therefore, interpretations and conclusions must be made in light of these qualifications.

Characteristics of Respondents

It is not difficult to construct a composite picture of these individuals. The respondents were predominantly white persons (89%); many were college dropouts (56%) who joined their groups between 1972 and 1975. Most described themselves as coming from middle-class (53%) or upper middle-class (22%) backgrounds. A majority of the sample was male (61%), a fact that may reflect a greater proportion of male participants in these particular movements (see Barker, 1984:10; Bromley and Shupe, 1979:94; Daner, 1976:68; Judah, 1974:86-87). Most persons (71%) initially joined between the ages of 18 and 23. In terms of religious upbringing or background, 41 percent were Catholic, 41 percent were Protestant, and 9 percent were Jewish. However, 86 percent described their prior religious affiliation as nominal. A majority of the individuals were already "searching" at the time of their conversion to the movement (74%). The sub-samples of defectors and members were well matched, exhibiting no marked differences among the background variables, perhaps with the single exception of age at joining. Defectors were slightly younger (x = 20.1) than members (22.3) at the time of entry, though the difference was not statistically significant. Overall, the data are consistent with previous research on the membership composition of these groups (tables are supplied for the reader in appendix B).

Objectivity and Subjective Accounts

What people experience and how they later interpret their experiences are often very different. I refer here to the problem of "biographical reconstruction" (Berger and Luckmann, 1966:159-60). As people form new social bonds and identify with new reference groups, they tend to interpret past experiences in ways that are meaningful to them in their current situations or milieux. Beckford (1978) has made this point with regard to biographical accounts of defectors from the Unification Church. He argues that actual accounts by defectors are often developed *post facto* in a negotiation process involving one's family and friends. In other words, "accounts given by actors of their own experiences are not to be simply taken as external descriptions of the situation they find themselves in, but are *part of the situation itself*" (Beckford, 1978:105). Individuals may internalize or incorporate definitional aspects of the new plausibility structure in the account in order to legitimate the departure. Consequently, he suggests that "qualitative and evaluative aspects of a supposedly descriptive account must be sensitively explored" by the researcher (Beckford, 1978:105).

The same problem arises in research on conversion to religious groups or movements. In a study of conversion to a fundamentalist communal organization, Richardson, et al., (1979:299-300) note that members' accounts of their lifestyles and behavior prior to conversion are often susceptible to "negative boasting"—the exaggeration of how sinful one was before he or she was converted. In the social system of the communal organization, the previous level of "spiritual darkness" is an important indicator of how "far" a person has come in the transformation to a new identity. Thus, persons whose past biographies feature greater levels of spiritual darkness are accorded more prestige by others. Biographical reconstruction is a pervasive problem in research of this type. It is not likely that one can expect to gather purely impartial accounts of stayers or leavers.

However, despite the liabilities of biographical accounts, these must be taken seriously. There is no practical alternative. But there are precautions or safeguards one can exercise while conducting interviews. I have endeavored to employ a strategy that was both "sensitive" and skeptical. The interview situation allowed me to explore these accounts at considerable length, and to probe for important factors that may have been overlooked or omitted by respondents. The theoretical propositions generated in this study provided some direction to questions and probes. In addition, the interviews were conducted with a structured questionnaire using numerous forced-choice items. This allowed me to gather uniform data on a large variety of attitudinal and behavioral details which called for less interpretive responses. In some instances, these provided important clues in piecing together a more comprehensive record of related events and experiences.

It is true, as Beckford (1978:105) and Skonovd (1981:22) point out, that defection accounts are only partially understood by the respondents because their newly acquired perspectives often obscure the process. The same principle applies when considering accounts of conversion. One's actions may take on new meaning in the light of a new identity or worldview. But the way in which the individual's new identity and perspective impinge upon the defection account is also an important aspect of this study. I will argue in chapter seven that one's new social location plays a crucial part in helping to finalize the disengagement process. We would expect defectors to see past experiences through the eyes of a new social world. But these accounts still remain a rich source of information about how such transformations occur. In essence, I have felt obliged to take these accounts seriously, yet not before subjecting them to skeptical inquiry and critical examination. Various items in the questionnaire were cross-checked for consistency and probes were used extensively when accounts appeared contradictory, ambiguous or unclear. When possible, details identifying specific places, events, or people were verified as well. In some cases, I obtained journals or diaries in order to supplement or corroborate verbal accounts. Interviews were taped to prevent the loss of significant data, and occasionally follow-up interviews were conducted when elaboration or clarification was required further.

PART TWO
PATTERNS OF DEFECTION

CHAPTER FOUR

PRECIPITATING FACTORS IN THE DEFECTION PROCESS

The process of disengagement from a movement must begin somewhere. It would be fair to say that doubts probably arise for most members on a regular basis. Commitment and adherence are dynamic and thus subject to occasional fluctuations or deflations that are routinely experienced but are not detrimental. Yet, there are some factors or influences that play a more critical role than others because they trigger major disconfirmation or disillusionment. These factors are sufficient to disrupt and suspend normal mechanisms of commitment maintenance. They generate a significant level of dissonance, destabilize one's plausibility structure, and initiate withdrawal. The propositions examined in this chapter identify the primary factors that set the defection process into motion.

Social Insulation

The less the degree to which a world-transforming movement provides effective insulation from the larger society, the greater the likelihood of defection. Insulation is an attempt by the movement to strategically create and maintain the most conducive conditions for intensive socialization.[1] Proposition one assumes that insulating boundaries will keep members away from adverse evaluations of the movement while internally promoting cohesion, conformity, and commitment. To the degree that these commitment-building processes are successful, the threat of defection declines. Conversely, the likelihood of defection increases when insulating boundaries are diminished or disrupted.

The most important means through which insulation in a world-transforming movement is disrupted is by prolonged separation of a member from the group. Data for this study show that persons who were separated from a world-transforming movement for a prolonged period of time were less likely to return to the group. Of the twelve persons who reported separation and isolation from other members for a period of three weeks or more, only four (33%) continued as committed members. On the other hand, the remaining eight (67%) pointed to the time spent apart from the movement as critical to their decision to leave. These individuals found that increasing time spent away from fellow believers and the ordinarily stable, reality-supporting measures of the religious group perpetuated doubts and uncertainties about their future involvement. One such account was given by a former member of the Unification Church who was accidentally separated from the group.

When I was in Vermont, I couldn't fundraise because I was Canadian, so I went up to Canada. I took a bus up and stayed with some Canadian people for a few days and then took the bus back. It sort of gave me more freedom and I could travel *incognito.* I wasn't a Moonie because I wasn't with a group of them.

When I really started questioning was when I was refused entry back into the States. They wouldn't let me back in, so I went back and stayed in Montreal for awhile. I finally got in touch with my team leader and he told me to hang on and they would take care of it. So while I was there I went over to McGill University and spent a lot of time in the library just reading.

I really just wanted to go back to school. At that point, I was really questioning: Was it right? (Interview #23).

This ex-member, whom I will call Gene, had been a full-time member of the Unification Church for a year and a half at the time of his departure. He was separated from his fundraising team through somewhat unusual circumstances, and was given a brief leave of absence while other members completed their activities. Gene was reunited with the group several weeks later but remained in the Unification Church only a few months before leaving. He admits to having some doubts prior to the protracted separation, though he places the turning point at the particular span of time spent apart from the group.

Isolation from one's group can act to disrupt or impede socialization and commitment-building processes which lead to defection. Of course, it is assumed that most members experience some disenchantment along the way. Some go on to face doubts with renewed vigor and self-sacrifice, seeing them as temporary distractions or even obstacles which are placed there by the divinity in order to test one's faith (Gerlach and Hine, 1970:172). But persons who defect from these movements are more likely to have had their normal doubts accelerated or greatly intensified through the perception of disconfirming evidence that gives credence and substance to their apprehensions (Richardson, *et al.*, 1981:12). In Gene's case, doubts emerge out of an extended period of separation from the movement. The effects of separation produce a decision, and the process of defection is set into motion, described by Gene in the following manner.

When I made up my mind in Montreal to go back to school, I sort of started maneuvering myself back to London, Ontario, where I originally lived when I went to the university. And, fortunately, they were starting a center there. So they said, "ok," you know, we will let you go back to London and help start a center. And, when I did go back to London I started seeing a lot of friends that I had known over the years, and it gave me a different perspective. I started to see things differently, and when they talked to me they would want to know, "What are you doing?" and "Why are you doing it?" You know, we would talk about it, and it's not like they really tried to persuade me, but at the same time, it was having a strong effect.

If commitment is basically a process by which individuals come to see group ideals and goals as self-expressive, then defection or deconversion is essentially a process by which individual self-expression comes to be divorced and detached from group ideals. The pursuit of private or extra-group interests involves a reordering of priorities that introduces marked conflict with collective purposes. Private interests are much less likely to emerge in the midst of a highly regulated and highly insulated milieu such as is found in a world-transforming movement. The process of detachment is more likely to arise when insulating boundaries are removed and individualistic expression is not tempered or regulated by organizational constraints.

The following case represents an example of how the removal of insulating boundaries can facilitate defection by allowing the growth of private interests. Lisa, a former member of the Children of God, attributes her decision to leave to an extended separation when she returned from Europe for a visit.

RESPONDENT: I guess it was actually just the amount of time I spent away from them (Children of God), and seeing that I actually wanted to stay away and live my live with Roger, doing the best on our own. . . .

When I first came home to visit after Roger had already left, my parents asked me if I wanted some furniture and confronted me with what I was going to do. Out of the blue, I just decided to go ahead and take it, and I called Roger and asked him to find a place for us to live in Boston.

INTERVIEWER: So when did you make the firm decision to leave?

RESPONDENT: I made the decision to get a place with Roger a few weeks after arriving back in the States for a visit. But it wasn't until the following December that I made up my mind that things were wrong with the Children, and that I didn't want to be a part of them. There was nothing specific that brought me to that conclusion, I just began to see, and let myself see, things clearer and from a different perspective. One thing interesting is, the decision really had to come from me. Whenever Roger tried to push his feelings on me it had a bad effect and made me hold tighter to the past. (Interview #7).

Lisa returned to the U.S. for a brief visit with her family and with her husband Roger, from whom she had separated the year before. While on leave, she stayed at her parents' home and purportedly had full intentions of returning to the movement. But after two weeks, her parents took the liberty of confronting her about future plans and goals, and about her marriage to Roger, and attempted to persuade her to stay by offering her furniture. Lisa responded by accepting the furniture and calling Roger in an attempt to reconcile their differences (Roger had defected and was opposed to the movement, though not vehement.) During this period, Lisa reported struggling with divided loyalties: she had strong ties to the movement ("The Family") and to her own family. But as time spent apart from the movement increased, the effects of socialization were eroded (". . . I just began to see, and let myself see, things clearer and from a different perspective") and an alternate plausibility structure adopted.

It could be argued that Lisa's defection was influenced more by a loyalty to her husband than by the absence of insulating boundaries. There can be no doubt that Lisa's marital tie to Roger was one factor in the decision-making process. Yet Lisa suggests that her husband's efforts to influence her decision had an adverse effect. Also, it must be taken into account that the Children of God discourage "private marriage ties [that] interfere with . . . Family and God ties," and that "they can be abandoned for the Glory of God and the good of the Family" (Berg, 1976:1367). Such teaching militates against two-person intimacy and loyalty. Since Roger and Lisa met and were married *after* they joined the Children of God, it is certain that these teachings and principles shaped their marital expectations.

Lisa was a full-time member of the Children of God for four and a half years. Thus, it is not surprising that she struggled with her decision to defect for almost a year after separation from the movement. Lisa's commitment was forcefully demonstrated by her choice to remain with the Children of God when her husband left. Her decision not to return came only after the insulating boundaries were removed and a prolonged separation eroded the bonds of commitment.

Both Lisa and Gene attributed their defection to the time spent apart from the movement. Both made critical decisions affecting their continued involvement after only a few weeks of separation. In Gene's case, the decision to leave came sooner, the whole process of deconversion lasting about two and a half months. For Lisa, the process was of greater duration and involved a greater personal conflict. These differences may be accounted for by differential lengths of commitment and Lisa's affective tie to her husband. These and other factors frequently enter the picture to modify and shape the intensity and duration of deconversion so that individual case histories will vary in detail and interpretation. Therefore, while the breakdown of insulating boundaries plays an important role in setting the process of defection into motion, many persons will experience different "trajectories" of transformation (Richardson, 1977a, 1977b).

World-transforming movements employ insulating boundaries as a rule. Under certain circumstances, however, these boundaries may be relaxed. One such instance is reported by a former member of the Children of God who was permitted to return home immediately after the Jonestown tragedy in 1978. Mindy received a letter from her mother expressing deep fears and anxieties about her involvement with "another Jonestown cult." She was allowed to return home after Moses David issued a letter stating that some members may have to visit their parents to reassure them of their safety. Mindy was the only person to leave her colony. She describes below the difficulty of leaving in the atmosphere of collective disapproval.

RESPONDENT: My mother sent some money, and there was a letter that came out from Moses David that said, "Go visit your family, if you have to." That's why I did it. You know, Jonestown had just happened. So I just left (Greece). It was really a hard thing for me to get out because people didn't want me to go. Really, nobody was encouraging it at all, and I had two kids. And it was just like crazy trying to get out of there. I didn't have a car. I had to leave all my things behind, and, you know, all my literature that I had read for years for fear that it would be confiscated at the border. The plane flight came through and somebody came and got us and took us to the plane. When we arrived here, my mother met us.

INTERVIEWER: Were you thinking about leaving, defecting?

RESPONDENT: No. You feel that it's God's will you're in. So to leave it, you know, was like crazy (Interview #35).

Mindy's decision not to return to the Children of God was facilitated primarily by her separation from the movement.

INTERVIEWER: So what happened when you arrived home?

RESPONDENT: I was greeted by my mother. I was still convinced that I belonged in the Children of God and it was really hard for me to function. You know, I felt like a fish out of water or something. I didn't have any of this literature with me (Mo letters) that I depended on for so long. But I wanted to visit my family here and I had intentions of going back to the group. My family confronted me and said, "Look, you know, Moses David is really insane," and they encouraged me to stay, and they were very loving, but I felt that they were wrong. So I just didn't worry about it.

But later, I just realized that if there were no other Christians outside the

Children of God, then how can anyone be right, right? I thought God was more than all that, you know. He had to be. So I just stayed, and my family supported me and my kids, and I just searched the scriptures and took a chance at finding a Christian person who might be a real Christian, and stuck in God's word for three months. After those three months, I made a decision that I had to stay where I was; though I hadn't faced half of it yet. But that was just my decision.

Mindy had been a full-time member with the Children of God for five and a half years. She met them in Greece while traveling through Europe in the summer of 1973. She joined three days after her initial contact with the movement. She never saw her parents nor returned home until she defected in January of 1979. She had no intention of defecting when she returned home to California. However, the social and psychological impact of her separation from the Family was demonstrated after only a few weeks when she voiced doubts about the special moral status of the movement. These doubts led to an extended three-month leave of absence from the group and self-expressed desire to find and develop a social relationship with persons of similarly high religious convictions.

Maintaining insulation is essential to the ongoing process of commitment-building in world-transforming movements. Competing loyalties and options are diminished by putting social distance between the group and one's other commitments. Insulation provides the kind of symbolic and social demarcation that reduces the chances of taking up excluded choices while it stresses the separateness and special uniqueness of group membership. Other possible courses of action become increasingly remote, less concrete, and more difficult to initiate the longer one continues to "invest" personal resources in the movement (Becker, 1960:35; Kanter, 1972:70-71).

At the level of interaction, the reduction or removal of insulation entails the disruption of ongoing relationships which are the vehicles of meaning and values. The disruption of social interaction impedes the channels of meaningful communication upon which socialization and commitment depend. Elsewhere, McHugh (1966) argues that some form of social disintegration must accompany desocialization of persons from total institutions such as prisons. McHugh (1966:359) even advocates intentional or "operant disintegration" of prison subcultures in order to expedite desocialization of inmates.

From a cognitive standpoint, when insulating boundaries are interrupted or dissolved, the basis for discrediting the larger social order is subverted. Clearly delineated boundaries function to separate and polarize insiders and outsiders, the just and the corrupt, the elect and the lost (Coser, 1974:5). The removal of these boundaries minimizes such distinctions and undermines the value of belonging to a unique group. In other words, uniqueness is only translated as "electedness" by others who share that perspective. Increased interaction with nonmembers who do not share that view introduces normative ambiguity due to nonreciprocity (Gouldner, 1960), and uniqueness becomes seen as an oddity. Mindy's comment that she "felt like a fish out of water" is a good illustration of displaced uniqueness. In the absence of mutual affirmation of her beliefs or worldview, the value of membership is thwarted.

The above cases of Gene, Lisa, and Mindy illustrate some typical examples of defection brought on by the disruption of insulating boundaries. But what about those who remained with the movement? How do they differ from those who left? In what ways can we explain their continuance despite separation? These cases also deserve some attention.

The four persons who stayed with the movement included two couples, both with the Children of God. One of the couples, Curt and Marcy, had experienced almost a year's separation. In actuality, it was not total separation. They were in constant touch with the movement. Moreover, this period of separation was interrupted by periodic visits with members passing through the area. Some of these stayed for as long as a month at a time. The reason for the separation was mainly a pragmatic one. Marcy had become pregnant while in Central America and the couple had decided to come back to the U.S. to have the baby. At the time of the interview, Curt was working at the telephone company in an effort to earn enough money for the couple to return to Central America.[3] They expressed a desire to join a small group of friends whom they had kept in contact with since their departure. As Curt remarked,

We're just staying as long as it takes to make some traveling money and then we are headed south. The Lord is really doing some great things down there and we know some brothers and sisters we can hook up with when we get there (Interview #91).

The other couple, Jerry and Okemi, had just returned from Japan for a brief visit. Jerry had married Okemi, a Japanese member of the group, while in that country. Because of the distance and the organizational demands, Jerry rarely had the opportunity to come back to the States. Nonetheless, they had managed to get a leave of absence and were in contact with Curt and Marcy at the time of their stay in New England. They remained in the country for four weeks and then returned to Japan.

There are at least two factors which distinguish these couples from the others and may help to explain why they remained with the movement. First, three of the four individuals who continued with the organization had tenures far exceeding those of the defectors. Curt, the veteran, had been with the Children of God for eleven years. He joined in Los Angeles in 1970, when the movement was just beginning. Marcy had been with "The Family" eight years, and Jerry seven years. Only Okemi was a relatively young member, having joined only four years prior to our meeting. The average length of membership for "stayers," then, was about seven and a half years. On the other hand, the average tenure for defectors was only about three and a half years.

This suggests that length of time in the movement may help to offset or neutralize the effects of separation. As argued earlier, alternative courses of action become increasingly remote and more difficult to initiate, the longer one continues to invest personal resources in the movement. As one's psychic investments in the group build, withdrawal is more costly. Stated in another way, the interruption of socialization processes is less likely to be damaging to the long-time member than to the novice.

A second factor which may help to explain why some persons stay, despite separation from the movement, is found in the marital tie. Both couples who remained were married after they joined the movement. Their individual devotion and loyalty to the movement was already established, and their marriages were fully approved by the leadership. This essentially means that, in the eyes of the leadership, their marriages would not detract from, or interfere with, their commitments to the group. Unlike the case involving Lisa, both parties in the two marriages had their commitments intact when separation from the group occurred. The distinct advantage of such an arrangement is that during a period of prolonged separation from the movement, one's spouse is also a fellow member who may help sustain group beliefs and identity. Thus, the individual is not entirely isolated. Though separated from the organization, the individual may continue to draw ideological and emotional support from his or her spouse/co-believer. Other than Lisa, none of the defectors here had a marital tie.

To summarize the findings, then, the data suggest preliminary support for proposition one. Persons who experience extended periods of separation from the movement are likely to languish and eventually withdraw altogether. The data show that eight of twelve persons who were separated from the group for three weeks or more left. However, the potential impact of insulation breakdown appears to diminish the longer members remain and upon the event that they marry after joining. The combination of these factors may be said to account for members staying despite the experience of prolonged separation.

Dyadic Exclusivity

The less the degree to which a world-transforming movement eliminates exclusive two-person intimacy, the greater the likelihood of defection. Two-person intimacy drains emotional energies away from the group because the many intersecting relations that may influence the individual (social control) are reduced in the case of dyadic involvements. Simmel (1950:123-24) has argued that in a dyadic involvement, one relationship is intensified at the expense of others. Thus, the greater the emotional involvement in the dyad, the more likely that other social relationships will be weakened. Specifically, Slater suggests that two-person intimacy increases "cathectic withdrawal" from other obligations to the social group. He identifies the inverse relation between two-person intimacy and group cohesiveness as it relates to groups that make high demands on their members.

Given this inverse relationship between dyadic cathexis and societal cathexis, another correlation suggests itself. We may hypothesize that the more totalitarian the collectivity, in terms of making demands upon the individual to involve every area of his life in collective activity, the stronger the prohibition against dyadic intimacy. . . .

Extreme prohibitions are also characteristic of utopian communistic communities, religious and otherwise, such as the Oneida experiment. In some instances, the dyadic intimacy prohibition is enforced at the same time that sexual promiscuity is encouraged, thus clearly revealing that the basis of the proscription is not fear of sexuality but fear of libidinal contraction—fear lest the function which the (group) performs for the individual could be performed for each other by the members of the dyad (Slater, 1963:349).

World-transforming movements are faced with the task of regulating sexual relationships in order to extract and maintain intense commitments from members. Though marriage is permitted in all three groups examined here, each group exercises strict controls over mate selection, marital lifestyles, childrearing, and sexual intimacy. When dyadic involvements are not subordinated to the group, withdrawal by one partner is more likely to influence the other to do the same.

Data for the study reveal that eight persons left specifically because their spouse or mate intended to leave the movement. On the other hand, none of the current members interviewed had a spouse or mate leave. Therefore, all persons who had a dyadic partner defect (seven couples including Lisa and Roger) ended up leaving the movement also. Any conclusions must be drawn carefully because of the small number of cases involved. Nonetheless, some explanation of these data are in order. The findings seem to suggest that if and when members have a spouse/mate who intends to leave, the other is more likely to leave also. However, the low incidence of this type of defection—only eight of forty-five cases (18%)—suggests that world-transforming movements are reasonably successful in regulating sexual relations in order to deter dyadic withdrawal. This is done primarily by requiring endogamous marriage—and then only after members have demonstrated a sufficient period of loyalty to the movement. For example, the Unification Church demands a three-year oath of celibacy before unmarried followers are eligible to be "matched" (i.e., engaged) by Reverend Moon. Interviews with movement leaders reveal that persons already married when they join are expected to separate and adopt a celibate lifestyle for a minimum of seven months in order to prove their faithfulness to the church.[4]

The data, however, indicate that the overwhelming majority of persons who joined these movements were single (87%). Therefore, previous marital ties probably pose less of a problem than might be expected by the mere fact of their relative infrequency. Nevertheless, when married couples do join world-transforming movements, these groups face a more difficult task in curtailing dyadic ties in order to increase group commitment. Of the six couples who entered these movements as marrieds, four left. This suggests that the apparent success that world-transforming movements have, in regard to the small number of dyadic defections, may be due to a high proportion of converts who are single. Unmarried persons do not have to dismantle strong dyadic commitments and thus, the movement is faced only with the problem of prevention, or regulation of intimacy. In any case, dyadic ties that are least subject to group controls present the greater threat of cathectic withdrawal. These would include 1) couples already married when joining, and 2) single persons who become emotionally involved without the knowledge or consent of the movement leadership.

Occasionally, unmarried members become emotionally attached and form dyadic commitments without the knowledge or consent of the group and its leaders. Under conditions where there exist insufficient constraints, ordinary interaction may lead to "exclusive" attachments that simply go unnoticed by other members. Though movement ideologies strictly forbid unregulated "private ties," long hours of mixed gender association through fundraising or recruitment activities may give rise to unintended emotional involvement. Members who find themselves in this predicament face an agonizing dilemma. Since dyadic arrangements are solely selected and regulated by the movement, the couple will most likely be asked to separate. Thus, the persons involved must choose between the group or the dyad.

One such account of an emotional attachment leading to a dyadic defection is given by a former member of the Unification Church. Sandy and her husband Paul met while fundraising. They were both members of a large musical group sponsored by the church. The band was required to fundraise when it was not performing, and Sandy and Paul were assigned to the same mobile fundraising team. A short time later, they reportedly fell in love. Sandy explains, in detail, the course of events leading up to their exit from the movement.

RESPONDENT: The biggest thing was the fact that I met this guy . . . we were sent out to fundraise for the band and we got to know each other, and after a certain amount of time we fell in love.

INTERVIEWER: How much time?

RESPONDENT: I would say within a couple of months we were pretty far gone, pretty deeply in love. And that was very much frowned upon by the church. . . . You are not allowed to choose the person you want to marry because, according to their beliefs, you are not competent to make that decision. Only Reverend Moon is able to choose the perfect mate for you. Once you are married, according to their ceremonies and so on, you become a perfect couple and produce perfect children. So anytime you started to become involved with a person, that was usually cut off as soon as anybody found out about it.

We were in a unique situation in that we were out fundraising and he was the team leader and I was his assistant. So we had an opportunity to develop the relationship, whereas if it had taken place in another situation, it probably would have been squelched before it had a chance to even start. But by the time they really found out about it and everything, we were already pretty deeply in love, pretty emotionally involved. But what happened was that, first, they started telling us, "Well, you have to go for a certain period of time, like twenty-one days, without talking to each other. But we never did that. Then, eventually, after about four or five months, someone else saw us walking down the street holding hands and reported us to the person that was my particular superior at the time. So they gave us a choice. They gave me a choice of either leaving the movement immediately there in New York, without any money or means to get anywhere, or to be sent to California to be with a group out there that was witnessing. So I chose to go out to California. They gave Paul the same choice, only they were going to send him to Ohio. So he went ahead and bought his bus ticket and he didn't stop in Ohio but he went ahead and [came] out to California and got me out of the movement too, and we both left.

I believe that it would have been difficult for me to leave it it hadn't been for him because they tell you that if you leave the movement you are spiritually dead. And, you know, you might as well be dead. You can get so involved in it that it's hard to imagine a life outside of the movement. So if it hadn't been for Paul and myself falling in love, I probably wouldn't have left (Interview #17).

Sandy had joined the Unification Church in January of 1976, and was a full-time member for a year and a half prior to her departure. Paul had been a full-time member for two years. Before becoming emotionally involved, both persons fully intended to abide by the church's practice of an arranged marriage. However, their assignments as leaders to the same mobile fundraising team forced them into a situation of having to work more closely together than ordinarily would be expected. It is quite common in the Unification Church that team captains meet with their assistants in the evenings, after a day's fundraising activities have been completed, in order to tabulate and record incoming dollars and discuss strategies for the following day. This routine mode of interaction not only provided a vehicle for the development of dyadic attachment, but it also served to camouflage the relationship in the eyes of other members. After the dyadic attachment developed, over a period of several months, commitment to the exclusive relationship began to rival commitment to the movement, though neither person perceived it in this way. When told by the leadership to terminate their involvement, Paul and Sandy quietly refused. When the issue was forced upon them, to choose between the two commitments, the eventual outcome was a dyadic defection. This couple's story may be described as fairly typical of several others who became emotionally involved.

Kanter (1972:87) observes that "the exclusive attachments of love dyads interfere with group cohesion by generating jealously and hostility." Sexual relationships may become a source of competition, jealous infighting, and division among members if intimacy is not effectively regulated. For example, single members may object to the unequal investment of resources and energies made by dyads who choose to spend valuable time with each other rather than the group. Or, members who do not, or cannot, secure dyadic attachments may eventually resent those who do. Thus, exclusive attachments introduce certain inequities in the organization. Such inequities are harmful to the solidarity of the movement.

World-transforming movements institute practices that are intended to prevent or deter the formation of love dyads. These include celibacy, arranged marriages, and sexual pluralism or group marriage. Such practices serve to remove the individual's control over intimacy and, hence, over the likelihood of exclusive attachments surfacing. But, as with the case of Sandy and Paul, willing acceptance of group controls over intimacy initially is not a guarantee against an unintended romantic development. When such attachments arise, members may (perhaps naively) expect the movement leadership to make an exception by allowing the relationship to continue. This is indicated by Paul's later comments that the Unification Church was "hypocritical," showing a "lack of real love" by not permitting them to marry within the organization (Interview #18).

A similar case involves two former members of the Children of God who also fell in love and attempted to obtain permission from the leadership to marry. Catherine and Jeff were given the same choice as Paul and Sandy; either to separate or leave the movement. They chose to leave the Children of God in order to marry. However, they later attempted to rejoin the movement in Europe, but reported encountering too many pressures by the leadership to break up. They ended up leaving permanently after two months. Jeff describes the series of events preceding their defection.

RESPONDENT: They wouldn't let us get married. They had the authority to tell you anything. I mean, in other words, they had complete spiritual authority over your life.

INTERVIEWER: Didn't you have any other recourse?

RESPONDENT: Leave. That was it. As a matter of fact, that's why we chose to get married. They threatened us, they told us that if we did choose to get married against [their] counsel, as they put it, we would have to go out on our own. That meant we would be kicked out. I didn't know it but Catherine did. She had been around long enough, but she thought our marriage was more important, that we would get married and leave together. She trusted me. So we went out on our own and went to Europe. Then I said, well, I don't mind going out on my own but at least they have to help me learn the language or something. So that's why we tried to rejoin them in Berne. They did take us in reluctantly, but they were afraid not to.

INTERVIEWER: What do you mean?

RESPONDENT: Well, you see, the orders for us not to get married, or to try and split us up, had come directly from David Berg himself. That's why, we didn't know it, but that had been the deal. They tried to keep us from getting married, and then after we did, they tried to break us up. Partly because Catherine had been one of the original members of the David Berg family and she knew the inner workings and all that had gone on. They were still set on breaking us up when we rejoined them. They really pressured us for those couple of months, so we left (Interview #38).

The cases of both Jeff and Catherine[5] and Sandy and Paul suggest that dyadic involvements do, in fact, represent direct competition for members' primary loyalties. Dyadic commitments here tend to emerge as the primary attachments when these movements employ a test of commitment, the ultimatum. The ultimatum is simply a means of discovering the priorities of individual members whose primary loyalties are in doubt. Dyadic involvement presents a genuine threat to one's commitment to the group ("she thought our marriage was more important"). Therefore, world-transforming movements must discourage exclusive two-person bonds if they wish to secure total commitment from their members.

The cases I have discussed so far are examples of individuals who entered as singles and subsequently became emotionally involved without the consent of the leadership. Now let us turn our attention to a typical case involving a couple who were already married upon entry.

Bill and Denise left the Unification Church in 1977, but the decision was initiated solely by Bill. His wife, Denise, did not share his disenchantment with the church and her departure was primarily an effort to *preserve* their relationship. Denise recounts the reasons for her decision.

> It was more like the fact that we were married and because he had made that decision. I felt like our marriage, our relationship as a couple, couldn't go on if I stayed there and he (didn't). Because it would be very difficult, I would be traveling all over and, you know, it wouldn't be conducive to the relationship. So much of that whole life was just so right for me. And when Bill made a decision to leave, it was really difficult for me to understand what happened, you know, to the process of his relationship with the church. I guess I felt like it had somewhat deteriorated, or he felt like he could be more useful in a different capacity.
>
> Actually, I didn't like having to make a choice between something I really loved and someone I really loved. But it was clear to me that Bill was not flexible, he was not in a position to be flexible. He had made up his mind that this was what he was going to do and that was it. So, because I was in a position where I could be flexible, then I was. It wasn't so much that I wanted to leave, but just that I felt like our relationship merited the opportunity to grow and develop in a different capacity, which was what Bill was asking for (Interview #26).

Bill and Denise shared a strong marital commitment to each other prior to joining that was never effectively weakened and subordinated to the larger group. Their commitment to each other survived despite the fact that they were required to separate and live celibate for the entire two and a half years of their involvement. The willingness of this couple to submit their sexual relationship to group controls may seem like a contradiction to the claim that their dyadic commitment was never effectively subordinated to the organization. But the adoption of celibacy was mutually agreed upon as a temporary sacrifice that would later produce a better marriage. Bill's comments clearly indicate this to be the case:

> I didn't care much for the idea (of celibacy). But we felt like, in the long run, the church was going to be a boost to our marriage (Interview #25).

They both found the ideals of the Unification Church to be very attractive and their mutual understanding was that it would provide a spiritually healthier context for their marriage and their future family. One of the central teachings of the Unification Church involves the promised restoration of "perfect families" which subsequently are able to reproduce "sinless children," and thus populate the physical kingdom of God (HSA-UWC 1975:124-38). For Bill and Denise, the Unification Church represented not just personal, but marital or familial, salvation from a corrupt world where divorce and family dissolution are all too frequent.

Specifically, the commitment to the Unification Church made by this couple was based on a set of expectations about redeeming society and their marriage simultaneously. In one sense, their commitment *as individuals* was seen as a contribution toward the establishment of a better world. But it was also perceived as an act of furthering the marital commitment by achieving redemption of future family relationships. Group commitment and dyadic commitment were *not* seen as competing attachments or rival loyalties; they were initially seen as harmonious. However, as time elapsed, Bill came to see the two commitments as conflicting. He describes his own response to the conflict in the following manner.

At first, I was so busy traveling all over the country. But after two and a half years, I said to myself, "Hey, what is going on here?" It got to a point where I felt it had been long enough. I was at the point, I guess—well, I felt like I was doing some good things, and that they were doing good things too. But I felt like I needed to gain perspective in my own mind, in my own life, with my wife and myself (Interview #25).

When asked how they would have responded if the church or Reverend Moon had not recognized their marriage, both agreed that they would have been forced to leave. Denise, however, felt such a possibility was unlikely. She believed that their marriage would have been "blessed" by Reverend Moon in the near future. Bill, on the other hand, was unwilling to wait, and insisted that they leave the movement. In the end, Bill was intransigent and Denise's loyalty to her husband proved to be the stronger of the two commitments.

The response by Denise was typical of two other cases. Fran, an ex-Unification Church member, and Margaret, a former Krishna devotee, both followed their husbands out. The men, in both of these cases, left because of disillusionment with the leadership. Neither of the women wanted to leave, but opted to go with their spouses rather than remain without them. Of the two women, Margaret had the greater struggle. She had been a member for three years, while Fran was only involved for nine months. Margaret's account of her decision is remarkably similar to Denise's, as the following comments indicate.

David said he was leaving, that he couldn't take it anymore, and he wanted me to leave too. I thought he was sort of overreacting, but I could tell he wasn't going to change his mind. He was having some problems with the temple president. So I had to make a choice, whether I was going to go with David or not. That wasn't that easy, I want to tell you. I love him very much, you know, . . . but I was also very committed to the philosophy and to the people there and I really didn't want to walk away from all that. It was one of the hardest decisions I ever had to make (Interview #36).

Margaret left with David in August of 1975. Two years later they divorced but Margaret did not return to the movement. She considered that their disagreement over leaving had a part in the breakup of their marriage. However, she also said she would "do it again" because of her love for David.

You know, even when I look back, I don't know that I would have done anything differently. He was my husband, and I guess I would probably do it again if I was faced with that situation . . . (Interview #36).

Dyadic attachments which are established prior to entry in the movement increase the potential for withdrawal. When individuals enter as married couples, the chance of a defection-producing crisis arising is increased. In other words, one partner may leave by virtue of the other's disaffection. The disruption does not have to be experienced firsthand, as we have seen in the previous cases.

Of course, not all couples who entered the movement left. Two couples, one with the Hare Krishna movement, and the other with the Unification Church, stayed. The question raised then is, how are these cases explained? How do they differ from the others? A brief examination of these cases should help to distinguish the stayers.

Lama das and his wife, Vrana das, entered the Hare Krishna movement in 1972. Lama das was originally from Puerto Rico. He moved to New York City with his family as a child. He was training to be a dancer and actor when he met his wife in 1970. They were married that same year. Two years later they joined the Hare Krishna temple in New York. They had been members for eight years at the time of my interview with Lama das. According to him, neither spouse was discontented with the arrangement, despite regular periods of separation from each other, nor had either ever expressed a desire to defect.

The other couple, Wendy and Mike, had joined the Unification Church in San Francisco in the summer of 1974. They were married almost three years before entering the movement. Mike was a student at a local university and Wendy was working as a waitress in a restaurant. Mike was approached on campus by some members of the Unification Church and invited to a dinner. He and Wendy attended the dinner which was followed by a lecture on the church's philosophy. They reportedly were impressed by the group and the ideals they promoted. Mike and Wendy joined within a month of their first contact. They were required to separate and live celibate lives. At the time of the interview, they had been apart—except for occasional visits, telephone calls, or letters—for five and a half years. When asked how they felt about that, Mike gave the following reply.

> I know that must sound strange to you but we just feel like there will be plenty of time for us to be together in the future. Right now, it's important that we do God's work. We're happy, and God's going to give us all the strength we need (Interview #72).

The most obvious feature shared by these couples is that none of the spouses had ever forced a serious test of primary loyalties. None of the individuals here reported experiencing a crisis or disillusionment that might have led to one partner's withdrawal. Neither did anyone express a wish to leave now, or in the future. The potential problems posed by rival commitments, therefore, had been avoided or delayed to the extent that now such a test would be much less likely to produce dyadic defection.

Once again, the longer one invests time, energy, and resources in the movement, the more difficult it is to withdraw. In effect, these members apparently had developed attachments to the group that now outweighed dyadic ties or pre-existing marital bonds. Mike's comments, for example, indicate that his priorities are with the group ("Right now it's important that we do God's work"). The difference here appears to be that the movement was able to fend off a serious challenge of primary loyalties until a group cathexis was consolidated. The impact of separation is not unlike that which was discussed in the preceding section on insulation breakdown. Prolonged separation has the effect of weakening or neutralizing the relationship. In this context, the *intended* result of such an arrangement was that the dyadic tie was palpably vitiated and subordinated to the group.

In summary, there is preliminary support for proposition two. All persons in the sample who had a dyadic partner defect, left also. This involved seven dyads in all, though one individual (Lisa) did not give this reason for her departure and is not used as supportive evidence here. Thus, a total of eight cases may be said to fall in this category. Of these eight, four cases were single persons who became emotionally involved without the knowledge or consent of the leadership, and four were persons already married when joining. Both types of dyadic involvements signify private, exclusive bonds that are less subject to control and present a greater threat of withdrawing from the group.

The Imminence of Transformation

The less the degree to which members of a world-transforming movement perceive the regulation of their time, labor, lifestyle, and sexual conduct as an urgent necessity, the greater the likelihood of defection. This simply means that commitment to a world-transforming movement is likely to decline when the perception of *urgency* dissipates. Shupe and Bromley (1980:238) contend that "if individuals were to make extreme personal sacrifices to help usher in this new era, then such efforts had to be defined as spiritually indispensible." World-transforming movements claim to be privileged agents of imminent and total change. The special status of the movement as *the* agent of the new order is an important and attractive feature to potential recruits. New members typically come into the movement with high expectations of realizing a new world. Over time, however, these expectations of immediate and sweeping success are imperiled if the urgency of the mission is not maintained so that members are willing to continually make extensive sacrifices.

This proposition focuses upon the fact that people leave out of frustration or disappointment with the lack of success of the movement. A declining sense of urgency suggests a diminishing importance because the task at hand has been unfulfilled, or has been recognized as something that will take a greater amount of time and energy than originally believed. Thus, the impending transformation is temporarily postponed and, consequently, the goals of the movement appear more remote and unattainable. In the face of decreasing exigency, the necessity of extreme personal sacrifice seems less crucial.

The findings show that nine persons left for this reason. Defectors tended to voice complaints about the lack of change they were effecting in society, and about the failure to see any promising signs that things were going to change in the near future. Conversely, members rarely expressed complaints or frustrations about the "success" of the movement. Of course, the objection may be raised that members were not being entirely honest in their responses. I would suggest another explanation.

Members are provided with alternate interpretations of unfulfilled claims which are at least plausible enough to sustain commitment. This amounts to the successful "dissonance-management" tactic (Prus, 1976) of negotiating social reality. According to Prus (1976:127), dissonance is a "socially negotiable" phenomenon that is developed through collective input and interpretation. Acceptable explanations are constructed which put the movement in a positive light, and these are endorsed by the faithful.

It is not surprising, then, that members tended to exaggerate their growth and impact within society, while offering countless interpretations of current events as "proof" of the forthcoming transformation. Indeed, none of the current members could be singled out as voicing complaints about the progress of the movement. Even occasional remarks by members which could be construed as expressions of disappointment were vigorously restated and defended as peremptory statements by those who voiced them. "We have had our share of problems in this country," one Hare Krishna devotee stated, "but even through bad publicity people are still chanting the name of Krishna. . . . When people just mention the name of Krishna there is spiritual advancement" (Interview #63).

People who leave world-transforming movements for such reasons may continue to accept some of the beliefs and practices of the group. However, these beliefs and practices are seen in a less urgent time frame. Thus the individuals involved cannot continue to justify to themselves making the extensive sacrifices required of full-time involvement. Because the possibility of imminent change appears implausible, total commitment no longer seems necessary.

Bart, a former member of the Unification Church, left out of frustration with the inability of the group to bring about any significant degree of change in society. Frustrations were experienced intensely at the personal level, leading Bart to abruptly walk out of a center one morning never to return. His list of disappointments are expressed pointedly in the following account.

> I think a lot of people . . . left for personal reasons of frustration, like myself. I felt like I wasn't able to accomplish anything and I wasn't bringing in more people and that simply paying rent on a building wasn't actually changing the world, and that fundraising was really just to sustain the people in the center. We weren't growing and no one was really taking any interest in us and there was such a tremendous amount of bad publicity at that point. I think there were a lot of people who just got frustrated and said this isn't working and left. Not so much that these people have lied to me, or taken advantage of me, or what-are-they-doing-to-my-life type of thing. I think a lot of people left out of frustration more than anything else (Interview #31).

Despite Bart's repeated observation that "a lot of people" left out of frustration, other remarks in the interview indicate a failure to see this as an organizational problem. Instead, he interprets the frustration as a result of personal faults and weaknesses.

RESPONDENT: . . . It was frustration, a frustration with the fact that I was not changing anything or anybody. It was much more of an individual thing; it was much more me trying to come to terms with selfishness and unselfishness, giving and not giving, and why I can't reach anybody, and that type of personal feeling of frustration and lack of accomplishment. So I initially just said, look, hey, I am going up to New Hampshire for awhile, see you guys later. Then at that point, saying that if I go back nothing is going to change, nothing is going to be different, I have to get on with my life, but at the same time I am getting on with my life, I can still get on with my relationship with God. . . . I have no intention of becoming a full-time, live-in church center member again.

INTERVIEWER: Why?

RESPONDENT: As an individual, that was not a productive lifestyle. I was not able to bring people in. All I was able to do was raise money to help pay the rent.

INTERVIEWER: But that might be an important role.

RESPONDENT: Okay, it is and it isn't. I guess I'm saying that that's not valuable enough to make me live my life that way.

The frustration expressed by Bart is derived from the movement's failure to convey and maintain a sense of urgent importance about continued involvement in the face of *inevitable* resistance and rejection. Though Bart assumes personal blame for unsuccessful efforts at recruiting new members, there is a notable ambivalence expressed about the progress of the larger movement, over which he clearly has no control. For example, he observes that the *group* was not experiencing any growth and that the potential for growth appeared very dim. Obviously, Bart's remark that "a lot of people left out of frustration" suggests that it was not an individual problem but a collective one.

Disappointment is likely a common occurrence in world-transforming movements. They have had only limited success in the U.S. and generally have been stigmatized by the media and anticult groups. Against such public reproach, members must rely on the movement organization to provide a strong plausibility structure to support unconventional beliefs. The movements themselves must also maintain flexible and alternative explanatory schemes that account for unfulfilled claims, and they must effectively convey these to members.

The urgency of the mission must not be allowed to wane when immediate gains are not realized. For example, if recruitment is falling off, then the movement must convince its members that other equally important gains are being made and that the ideals of the group are being perpetually advanced. Indicators of progress or growth must be sought in other areas of organizational life so that widespread discouragement is thwarted. Success must be strategically redefined so that weaknesses become translated as strengths. One means of doing this is to claim a monopoly on "truth" while suggesting that only a chosen few will respond to the message initially. Remarks by a current member of the Unification Church illustrate the success of this type of strategy.

> People in the church have a greater capacity for love. We have truth. Anybody who really investigates the Principles honestly, with all their heart, will discover this. It's terrible out there. People are unhappy, there's no joy. Everybody's on edge, paranoid. This is the only sane place to be. . . .
>
> We may be small compared to other denominations, but look how far we've come in a short period of time. . . . It'll take awhile, but Reverend Moon has been given a mission by God to unify Christianity. The ones that are here now have been called to assist him. It's not going to be easy, but we have a unity of purpose (Interview #74).

As Prus (1976:127) suggests, dissonance in social or religious movements is socially negotiable. Therefore, when dissonance-reducing strategies or tactics are effectively employed, the likelihood of defection decreases. In Bart's case, no such alternative explanation or perspective is evidenced. Inability to recruit new members equals failure, and perceived failure leads to severe frustration and, ultimately, withdrawal.

A similar example involves a former devotee of the Hare Krishna movement. Bernie was a full-time devotee for about one year before leaving in 1977. His frustration grew out of a daily routine of austerity in the absence of any visible signs of movement growth or progress. According to Bernie, more persons actually left the movement than joined, indicating a dismal contradiction of prior claims to ushering in the "Golden Age." Against the perceived backdrop of stalled growth or stagnancy, Bernie describes the dissipation of fervor and commitment preceding his departure from the Hare Krishna movement.

RESPONDENT: It was very tough to lead that type of life; I mean it was very austere being celibate, being a Brahmacari. I didn't like being celibate and I didn't feel that if you wanted to attain God-consciousness it was necessary to do all the things they asked; you know, to go to those extremes.

INTERVIEWER: Why not?

RESPONDENT: Well, you know, I lived in the temple for a year and I followed the four regulative principles and I chanted sixteen rounds and I did sankraton and I did all those things. But you don't have to live in the temple to practice Krishna consciousness; you can do it on your own, at home. Krishna consciousness just means God-realization, being a servant of the Lord. Besides, there were some things I just didn't like about living in the temple. I felt that we should be preaching about Krishna more and spreading the philosophy. But there was so much emphasis on book distribution and getting donations from people any way we could. We even had quotas. . . . And I don't think most people ever read the literature anyway; they would just give a donation to get us off their backs. . . . Also, not that many people ever came around or joined while I was there. Devotees would come in from other temples, but I only saw a few people join the whole time I lived there. I think more people left than joined.

INTERVIEWER: How many left?

RESPONDENT: Oh, I don't know, maybe six or seven. And that's not the kind of thing you expect when you first become a devotee. Don't misunderstand me, I'm not putting it down, it takes a lot of dedication and self-discipline to be a devotee. But I just couldn't see giving my whole life to that. I guess I was just frustrated with the way things were in the temple (Interview #24).

The comments made by this ex-devotee point to demoralizing conditions at the temple that reflect unrealized ideals and goals. Bernie's discouragement was directly related to such conditions, giving rise to the perception that extensive personal sacrifices were not warranted by commitment to a stalled cause.

The perceived stagnancy of the movement described by Bernie parallels what Zald and Ash (1966:335) have referred to as a "becalmed movement." A becalmed movement is one which has created or found a niche in society, but its growth has slowed or ceased. Goal attainment is not expected in the near future, or, as in the case of world-transforming movements, the time-frame for completing the agenda is vaguely defined and ambiguous enough so that the prospective transformation appears within reach but is never actually achieved. A becalmed movement is vulnerable to a loss of emotional fervor among members, and therefore the leadership is faced with the problem of generating commitment incentives to curb apathy and discouragement. Both Bart and Bernie represent typical cases of individuals lost to the becalmed movement. The lack of growth and progress by these movements engenders disappointment while alternate explanatory schemes that account for unfulfilled claims are either absent or ineffective in preventing withdrawal.

When collective expectations are high, the group runs a greater risk in reconciling the discrepancy between touted claims and the mundane realities of a becalmed movement. The wider the disparity between initial expectations of imminent change and the practical experience of undetectable progress, the more likely it will lead to profound disillusionment, especially if the movement is not able to successfully persuade its members that gains are being procured in other ways. As I have already suggested, this involves the dilemma of cognitive dissonance, the need to integrate and harmonize disconfirming evidence (Festinger, 1957). Some previous research has shown that doomsday movements can be surprisingly resilient to disconfirming evidence, such as the failure of major prophesied events to come true (Cross, 1950/1982; Festinger, et al., 1964; Zygmunt, 1970). Nonetheless, while these movements have survived, it must not be overlooked that at least some members are *lost* in this process. Festinger, et al., (1964:205-208) describe from case studies two individuals who left a flying saucer cult after a prophetic event failed to materialize.[6] Cross (1950/1982:309) observes that defection from the Millerite movement was "substantial" after they unsuccessfully predicted the second coming of Christ in 1844. Even among those who remained, the confusion produced a number of schismatic sects.

In instances of prophetic failure, the movement must counter with dissonance-reducing strategies, including an effective reinterpretation of the disconfirmed prediction. But such an explanation is not always adequate to dispel doubts of all members, even when combined with such dissonance-reduction tactics as heightening or "dramatizing dissonance associated with leaving" (Prus, 1976:129). World-transforming movements characteristically employ tactics of warning, exhorting, or cautioning potential apostates of possible harm (divine retribution) associated with leaving. Individuals may be told that they are "turning their back" on God and be singled out as "backsliders."

Nonetheless, when faced with an unfulfilled prophecy, some members choose to resolve the dissonance by defecting. One such case involves a former member of the Children of God who left the movement after an unsuccessful doomsday prediction by the group's founder-leader, Moses David. In 1973, Moses David issued a "Forty Days" prophecy which predicted the comet Kohoutek would destroy America (Moses David, 1973). In the aftermath of the unfulfilled prophecy, Roger describes the impact upon his decision to leave.

> Initially, I would say the first big jolt was when Mo came out with this forty days prophecy about, you know, forty days and America would be destroyed. . . . We were in Germany when that came out and we believed that if Mo said it was going to happen, it was going to happen, you know? So we were in the streets warning everybody that in forty days America was going to be destroyed. And when the forty days went by and nothing happened . . . he came out with a letter that kind of explained things away. . . . At the time I kind of accepted it—but I kind of wondered about it inside. And then there were some people I met on the street, a few Germans, that said, "Up until the forty days prophecy came out I thought you all were right on, but I don't know anymore." That was probably the first thing that happened that made me start to question in my own heart whether or not everything was, you know, peachy keen.

> Then Lisa and I came back to visit our families. Lisa had some friends that were Christians that, when we visited them, really blasted Mo and called him a false prophet and just really told us in no uncertain terms that things were not all in order with the Family. And that was the first time I ever met anybody who had that strong of convictions about Mo's wrongness, that it really triggered me . . . (Interview #8).

According to Roger, the dissonance experienced after the unfulfilled prophecy was only partially resolved by the retrospective explanation offered by Moses David. The dissonance-reducing strategy of reinterpreting the initial prophecy was not adequate to offset doubts augmented by encounters with nonmembers who decried the disconfirmation. For Roger, the disillusionment leading to his defection laid in the arrest of anticipated success, the failure of a major prophetic occurrence that he believed would come to pass. His initial belief was betrayed as his efforts to convince others of the warning prophecy backfired.

Failure, whether associated with an unfulfilled prophecy or a becalmed movement, can lead to confusion, frustration, and eventually withdrawal. Of course, the perception of failure is socially negotiable and the continued survival of the Children of God attests to the fact that members may not interpret a disconfirmed prophecy as failure or contradictory evidence. But such a condition may create a greater vulnerability to membership losses and therefore the movement must maximize efforts of dissonance management to deter discouragement and disillusionment. These efforts can only be considered more or less effective. In Roger's case, an alternate explanatory scheme was only partially successful, and when contact with nonmembers fed already existing doubts, the result was defection.

Another defection involving the "Forty Days" prophecy was reported by a young woman. Jennifer was a full-time member of the Children of God for sixteen months before leaving in 1974. She traveled to London with other core members in 1973 to avoid the forthcoming holocaust predicted by Moses David. But when the event failed to take place, she lost faith and left. She gives the following account of her experience.

> I'd have to say that it was because of that whole thing with Mo's prophecy about the destruction of America. I was in London right before that happened. We were all passing out Mo letters like crazy trying to get the word out to people. . . . You know, we were so convinced that the tribulation was going to start, like it says in the Book of Revelation. . . . I sent copies to my parents, my sister who was in college at the time, and even to some old girlfriends.

> . . . So when the time finally came, nothing happened. I was really let down. I know Mo later said he didn't mean that America would be "literally" destroyed and all that. But that's what we told people when we handed out the literature. And after that they just laughed at us. I really felt silly. Maybe I was just naive but I really thought it was going to happen (Interview #5).

Perhaps the most serious problem introduced here was that the nature of the warning prophecy forced members to make the event open to empirical falsification by outsiders. Members were obliged to explicitly inform and forewarn nonbelievers of the impending catastrophe. Consequently, the ability of the movement leadership to successfully retract or reinterpret the prophecy, after it failed to materialize, was greatly weakened.

Because outsiders are not likely to accept retrospective explanations of unfulfilled prophecy, individual members may be subject to disparaging criticism that undermines conviction. It becomes more difficult for individuals to see total and uncompromising commitments as indispensible when disconfirming evidence cannot be exclusively redefined within the parameters of the group. Outsiders, no doubt, are likely to emphasize contradictions, thereby deepening the humiliation of the member. Jennifer and Roger both express sensitivity to the attitudes and opinions of outsiders which may account for their vulnerability in this situation. Roger, as I have already noted, credits the impact of several outsiders in his decision to leave. Jennifer implies the same in her reference to being laughed at ("after that they just laughed at us") and feeling "silly."

To summarize these findings, then, there is good preliminary support for proposition three. Nine defectors in the sample report leaving because of frustration or disillusionment with the movement to realize its claims. On the other hand, complaints among members about their success in accomplishing collective goals is virtually absent. In fact, current members tend to boast of their impact upon society. It is suggested here that since definitions of success are socially negotiable, people who leave are those for whom the negotiations are absent or inadequate.

Primary Group Affectivity

The less the degree to which members of the world-transforming movement perceive the organization as fulfilling the affective needs of a primary or quasi-primary group, the greater the likelihood of defection. Sociologists have argued that these movements attract youthful followers because they serve as primary or quasi-primary groups that create settings for interpersonal communal relations resembling extended family ties (Marx and Ellison, 1975; Richardson, *et al.*, 1979; Robbins and Anthony, 1981:214-16). Individuals are said to seek out these groups in order to meet affective needs in the context of a strong moral community (Doress and Porter, 1981). According to Robbins and Anthony (1981:215), new religious movements frequently are able to develop "communal fellowships which combine the diffuse affectivity or 'loving' quality of familial roles with universalistic symbols and meanings." Consequently, the movements may act to replace traditional mediating collectivities or quasi-primary groups, those groups that play a mediating role in the socialization process between the nuclear family and the larger society (e.g., the extended family, the traditional neighborhood, the church). They act to disengage youth from exclusive dependence upon the nuclear family for interpersonal relationships and value transmission. However, if and when interpersonal relationships among members of a world-transforming movement are perceived as indifferent, uncaring or unloving, disaffection is more likely to arise.

Intimacy and affectivity must be diffused throughout the entire group in order to realize the goals of unity, spiritual harmony, and group cohesiveness. Kanter has shown that certain organizational requisites, such as group singing, daily meetings, ceremonies or rituals, communal living, working and sharing help to develop a strong "we-feeling" among members and provide incentives for commitment (Kanter, 1972:91-103). In a very similar manner to the groups that Kanter studied, world-transforming movements utilize these requisites to encourage feelings of closeness and community. Kanter suggests that these are mechanisms that facilitate "communion." "Communion mechanisms develop equality, fellowship, and group consciousness which lead to the formation of a cohesive, emotionally involving, and affectively satisfying community" (Kanter, 1972:93).

Such a communal organization may suffer when overly rigid structures fail to allow for, or impede, development of meaningful and caring relationships. In a world-transforming movement, for example, emotional needs of members may be sacrificed for the higher goal of mobilizing needed funds and resources to keep the organization afloat. "Personal problems" may be interpreted as a result of individual selfishness and lack of faith, a failure to give one hundred percent. Therefore, when those primary relationships come to be seen as increasingly impersonal and unloving, individuals are more likely to become disaffected and leave.

The data here indicate a lack of support for proposition four. Only three persons in the sample of defectors reported leaving specifically for this reason. Indeed, defectors frequently pointed out that the quality and intensity of interpersonal relationships was one of the most positive aspects of their involvement. However, they also frequently distinguished between members and leaders—a distinction I will pursue in the next section. Among current members, the sense of unity and closeness with spiritual brothers and sisters was highly valued. When asked to describe how the movement was like or unlike a "family" to them, most of the present members could draw subjectively meaningful comparisons to their biological families, or to "ideal" family relationships. Rarely did members even offer descriptions of ways in which the movement was not like a family. One exception was given by a current member of the Unification Church.

Well, I didn't join because of the community, or because I thought somehow they could replace my real family. I joined because of the ideals. I spent sixteen years in Catholic schools and Christianity never really made sense to me until I met some people from the Unification Church who understood what they believed. I mean people here know what they believe. I'm sure some people join because of the community, at first, but that's not going to sustain them (Interview #70).

It would appear that world-transforming movements have been somewhat successful in generating and diffusing affectivity among their members. This holds true despite the numerous restrictions on personal freedoms and unusually high expectations of sacrifice required of individuals, and it holds true for both members and defectors. Beckford (1978:109) reports a similar finding among ex-Unification Church members: ". . . When I have questioned ex-members more closely about the way they felt toward their former colleagues 'during membership,' their answers have generally indicated that they felt nothing but love and admiration for them." Admittedly, the sentiments expressed by former members are usually embedded in very ambivalent attitudes about these groups. On the one hand, they tend to see these movements as misguided or spiritually adrift. On the other hand, they recall the closeness of relationships with other members with great fondness. For analytical purposes then, I find it necessary to distinguish between interaction at the level of interpersonal relations with fellow members and interaction with leadership.

Two explanations might be offered for the lack of support for proposition four. First it may be that *only* those members who join for reasons of fulfilling affective needs leave if those needs are not met. However, evidence for this hypothesis is not provided either. A measure of family closeness was employed in the questionnaire to assess the validity of affective deprivation of converts. It was found that 44 percent (N = 39, 17 defectors, 22 members) of the sample reported relationships with their families that were "not close." Of the seventeen defectors in this category, only two could be identified with the affective deprivation hypothesis described above. In other words, most of those who reported some degree of affective deprivation before joining the movement (i.e., lack of closeness to family), did not indicate leaving because of unfulfilled affective needs.[7]

Second, it may be that these movements are relatively successful in creating primary group settings so that persons who leave do so for reasons other than unfulfilled affective needs. Both these data and Beckford's (1978) suggest that even ex-members who emphatically disagree with movement policies or ideology still often describe their interpersonal experiences with other members in a positive light. Defectors tend to retain an admiration for the spirit of cooperation, harmony, and dedication among members who remain. This finding follows the same analytical distinction described earlier, and it accounts for Beckford's observation that attitudes expressed by ex-members towards their former groups are ambivalent. Communal groups provide unique settings for developing emotionally satisfying relationships amidst a world dominated by impersonal bureaucratic structures (Hillery, 1981). Therefore, despite other grievances voiced by persons who leave, it would appear that experiences of belonging to a close-knit community are generally perceived as gratifying.

In short, these data do not support proposition four. Rather they suggest that world-transforming movements lose few members because of a lack of felt-closeness or unrealized affective reciprocation. The reason for this appears to stem from their ability to develop and maintain communal fellowships that effectively diffuse intimacy.[8] We may assume, then, that this particular dimension of commitment constitutes a vital part of what limited success these movements have enjoyed.

Leadership

The less the degree to which members of a world-transforming movement perceive the leadership as "exemplary," the greater the likelihood of defection. Weber (1963:55) describes an "exemplary" prophet or leader as one who leads others down the same path of salvation he himself has traveled. The concept of exemplary leadership is modified and extended here to include actions by all leaders (the prophet leader and the secondary leaders) that are subjectively perceived as consistent with the ideals and goals of the movement. Oberschall (1973:146) contends that leaders "have to prove through personal sacrifice and example their commitment to the cause; they must create . . . faith among the rank and file." Wilson (1973:309) argues that commitment "has meaning for the individual only so long as his leader and those around him seem to warrant that loyalty. . . ." Commitment to a movement characterized by charismatic leadership thus emerges out of an investment of *trust* made by members. Most of the literature on charismatic leadership focuses on the individual personality or prowess of leaders. However, "[t]he other side of the charismatic relationship," Wilson (1973:204) says, "is that the followers have complete personal trust in the individual." Charismatic leadership must be recognized and validated by others who are willing to give up previous commitments and realign loyalties to the leader or leaders of the movement. One problem all world-transforming movements face is that followers need to be convinced that movement leaders are legitimate representatives or embodiments or moral truths and thus worthy of their sacrifice and dedication.

> The charismatic leader gains a following because he is thought to possess *exemplary* qualities which manifest themselves in feats of prophecy, divination, heroism, and exceptional endurance. The important thing to note, however, is that these qualities are imputed to the individual concerned by other people and are not intrinsic to his personality. Charismatic recognition is not tied, therefore, to particular universalistic personality attributes but is a function of both those qualities demanded or looked for by the group and the input made by the individual. *The particular qualities selected as being exemplary are those which are consonant with the group's goals* (emphasis mine, Wilson, 1973:202).

If, however, invested loyalty or trust is betrayed through actions that are perceived as morally inconsistent with espoused ideals or goals, the likelihood of defection increases.

Data for the study provided strong support for proposition five. Thirteen defectors from the sample pointed to unexemplary leadership as their primary reason for leaving. These ex-members reported disillusioning experiences with leaders which they clearly interpreted as ethically inconsistent, hypocritical, or immoral. On the other hand, current members rarely registered any complaints at all about the leadership. There were no reports of major disconfirming experiences such as was found among defectors. Current members typically affirmed the belief that their leaders were placed there by divine will, such arrangements being defined as legitimate and sacred. The following remarks by one member of the Hare Krishna movement serves as an example.

Prabhupada (Bhaktivedanta) was uncontaminated. He didn't talk about anything but Krishna. He didn't do anything but Krishna. He was totally clear. That's our aspiration, that we can become pure devotees like him. . . . The temple leader, he is here as our spiritual authority to help guide us toward Krishna consciousness, especially the younger devotees. He is more spiritually advanced, so there's a lot we can learn from his example (Interview #63).

Disillusionment may come through an invalidating experience with the prophet-leader or through secondary leaders. The latter constitute delegated authority who are responsible directly or indirectly to the prophet-leader. Weber (1963:60) notes that these secondary leaders "generally also possess some charismatic qualifications." Delegated leadership are seen as key personnel who carry out the prophet's directives for implementing the new social order (Wilson, 1973:206). They mediate and interpret the prophet's mission at the local level. Essentially, secondary leadership are indispensible because they serve as an important link between grass-roots followers and the prophet-leader. However, secondary leaders may become overzealous, harsh, or insensitive in their roles as delegated authority, thus exhibiting unexemplary leadership qualities. Such morally ambivalent behavior is more likely to alienate members and produce defections.

One example of a defection attributed to unexemplary leadership involves a former member of the Unification Church. Randy reportedly left the movement because of an interpersonal conflict with a high-ranking leader. Expressing misgivings about the harshness of their lifestyle apparently put Randy in disfavor with the leadership. After an unpleasant confrontation concerning the issue of discipline, he decided to leave.

RESPONDENT: There were certain leaders that I just didn't get along with. I didn't agree with the way they were going about doing things. I thought they were doing more harm than good, you know? I think that is where everything began.

INTERVIEWER: Could you elaborate just a little?

RESPONDENT: Well, I don't want to mention any names but I think that one of the problems that exists in the Unification Church is the fact that there are so many leaders from Japan that come in and take over. They are given high positions and they lead from a Japanese point of view, you know, which is hard for Americans to accept. At least it was for me. You know, I wasn't studying to be a "Ninja." The Japanese are a very, very disciplined people culturally, I think, and this was shown in their leadership which I thought was too harsh. . . . They just expected too much, they were too harsh.

There was one particular leader that I had run-ins with a few times. It was as if he told you something; he was so highly esteemed that he was one you never spoke back to. . . . But I just did not agree with him, and he knew it, and I was a thorn in his side. So things didn't go well between us. After one time I had a run-in with him, I just took off . . . (Interview #27).

For Randy, the authoritarian discipline of Japanese leaders was seen as intolerable, and "doing more harm than good." His reference to a "Ninja" vividly connotes the militaristic style of leadership he found too harsh and, hence, not consonant with other ideals within the movement such as love, solidarity, and camaraderie. The perception of unexemplary leadership qualities among the transplanted Japanese fueled a growing and unresolvable conflict for Randy that led to an increased alienation from the movement. In effect, the "run-ins" with these leaders served to progressively loosen ties to the group and set the stage for a final confrontation which immediately preceded his departure.

Another case involving a disillusioning experience with secondary leadership is recounted by two former members of the Children of God. Carl and Susan were told by the local leadership to take their infant out with them while "litnessing" (witnessing through literature distribution) despite the severe cold weather. When the child developed a cold, Susan reportedly refused to take the child out again. As a result, the colony leaders interpreted her actions as "backsliding," which created further repercussions and fed a growing friction between the couple and their commitment to the group. Susan gives the following account of the incident.

> It was the leaders that I got real dissatisfied with; the way they were treating people. . . . Our little boy was about four or five months old and the weather was really cold in Oklahoma City; it was really windy there. So when it was thirty degrees with the wind blowing, it makes it almost zero. . . . It was so cold that finally one day I just refused to go. I said, "I'm not going to take him out in this weather. He has had a bad cough and a cold and all this." So, wow, the leaders just got so mad at me. They really didn't like anyone who was rebellious, but I still refused to go out.

> So after that, it was like all the leaders ganged up on us. They started talking behind our backs, and they said I was backsliding. . . . They really hurt my feelings because they were saying all these things that weren't true. We really wanted to leave right then and there, but the regional leader came by and he saw our situation and he wanted us to go out and start a new colony in Wichita Falls. So we thought that if maybe we went off and started a new colony, we would have more freedom and we wouldn't have any other leaders over us all the time. But once we got out to Wichita Falls our hearts just weren't in it. Carl was really disillusioned with it. . . . We just decided [to leave] after that (Interview #14).

In this case, Susan and Carl's trust in the movement leadership was violated. The colony leader's lack of genuine concern for their sick child was perceived as callous. They could not reconcile the insensible demands that threatened the health of their child with their expectations of exemplary leadership. Nor could they understand the subsequent retaliatory behavior of the leadership after they refused to comply. These actions were seen by Carl and Susan as a betrayal of the group ideals to which they were committed—community, mutual concern for others, and love.

In some instances, organizational *goals* may conflict with movement *ideals*. For example, in the above case the goal of mobilizing needed funds superseded all other concerns. The leadership, because of their positions of responsibility, were almost exclusively goal-oriented, to the detriment of collective ideals. The problem of goal-attainment led them to redefine the conflict as simply a matter of faith. Carl had the following comments about the conflict.

> It was one of the old COG standards of having faith; you know? You don't have to have common sense, as long as you have faith you can take the baby out and stick him in the snow—just as long as you have faith. But I didn't really like the idea. He got really sick and we took him to the hospital and it was kind of looked down upon. But I thought, well, you reap what you sow and if you don't have

enough good sense to wear clothes in cold weather, if you don't have enough sense to leave a baby in the house in cold weather, you are going to get a sick baby, and it's not a matter of faith, it's just a matter of reaping what you sow; it's common sense (Interview #12).

Efforts at dissonance management by the movement leadership centered largely on the issue of faith. The perceived ethical contradiction of exposing a sick infant to inclement weather in order to fundraise was strategically defined by the colony leaders as a "test" of faith. But this dissonance-reducing tactic proved unsuccessful as the couple found alternate scriptural support for their desire to protect their child.

The previous examples examined the conflict arising from invalidating experiences with secondary leadership. But the problem is brought into sharper focus when one looks at the dissolution of the relationship between a disciple and the prophet-leader after the latter exhibits unexemplary or morally ambivalent behavior.

Ethan, a former devotee of the Hare Krishna movement, recounts a dissonance-creating experience when the prophet-leader, A. C. Bhaktivedanta, responded to an organizational problem in an unanticipated way.

About 1975, we started getting these letters from India saying there is going to be a change. Now the guru tells us that we got to stress book distribution because if the person on the street gets a book, he is getting Krishna. He said, "Don't bother wasting time preaching on the street. My books are so potent that if they read one page their lives will be changed," because he is a pure devotee. We are such mudhas (asses), if we preach for half an hour it is useless. But if he speaks one sentence, it will go right to their hearts and change their lives. So we were told to get out and sell books.

Well, it wasn't too long after that that things started getting out of hand. Devotees were trying so hard to sell books they began using deception, transcendental trickery.

. . . Then finally, in 1976, we wrote a letter to Prabhupada saying, "At the airport girls are cheating. While in line they are stealing servicemen's wallets. All these things are being written up in the newspapers." We sent one of the newspaper clippings to India thinking that the guru was going to read this and straighten everything out. He was going to see all this and put a stop to it. Things had really gotten out of hand and we just knew he was going to blow the whistle on the whole thing.

Well, a letter came back from India and he says, "This is very good. This man has said Krishna many times in his article. Therefore, when people read this article, they will be purified. It does not matter good or bad; all we are interested in is having the name Krishna implanted in people's consciousness. As far as these techniques are concerned, it's not important." Then he said, "The end justifies the means."

I couldn't believe it. I mean, I almost fell over. I remember thinking, this can't be. He can't say this. How can he say this? He is supposed to be a pure devotee: perfect, holy, and sinless, and he is saying that lying and stealing is not wrong? I just couldn't believe it. That just really burst my balloon (Interview #41).

For Ethan, this experience proved to be critical. His perception of Bhaktivedanta's integrity as an exemplary leader was severely damaged creating irreconcilable dissonance. As in the two previous examples, the actions of a leader (in this case the prophet-leader) violated the nature of the charismatic relationship built on trust. Trust here included a set of expectations that demanded consonance with such attributes as "holy, perfect, and sinless."

Indeed, the legitimacy of the charismatic leader derives from the perceived ability of the person to demonstrate unique qualities that set him/her apart as special or extraordinary and, therefore, deserving of the honor and esteem of members. With regard to secondary leaders, the perception of exemplary qualities justifies the position of authority and leadership within the movement. But when the authenticity of these imputed qualities is seriously questioned, the bond of trust becomes strained, increasing the likelihood of defection.

Skonovd (1981:92) suggests that commitment to this type of relationship is much like a "marriage." Wilson (1973:204) makes a similar observation in describing the charismatic relationship as a "love relationship." Generally, "followers show enormous respect and even love for their leader in a display of personality worship that is not manifest in other types of leadership" (Wilson, 1973:204). Consequently, in this type of relationship betrayal through morally contradictory behavior is analogous to a spouse who violates the marital commitment. The bond rests heavily on the element of trust, but when this trust is betrayed the relationship is likely to be damaged.[9]

Research suggests that American converts to new religious movements often have been motivated by the moral ambiguity they witnessed among dominant cultural institutions and values (Bellah, 1976; Doress and Porter, 1981; Robbins and Anthony, 1981). Therefore, it should not be surprising that observed inconsistencies between espoused ideals and actual practices by leaders of world-transforming movements would produce among some members the same disillusionment that motivated them to initially reject mainstream culture. Pavlos (1982:43) contends that "charismatic leaders have what psychologists label *credibility*, the perception by others that they possess expertise and trustworthiness." But as in the case of Ethan, morally ambivalent behavior by movement leaders destroys the credibility of the mission and robs the group of its special moral status precisely because it exhibits the same flaws one finds in the corrupted social order outside the movement.

These data provide good support for proposition five. Almost one third of the defectors in the sample attribute their withdrawal to unexemplary leadership. The cases of Randy, Susan and Carl, and Ethan are typical of persons who report leaving because of disillusioning experiences with leaders. Current members, on the other hand, are eager to affirm their confidence in movement leaders. Moreover, they often are quick to dismiss the claims of defectors and defend the actions of leaders. For example, after describing an incident of defection related to unexemplary leadership, one member of the Unification Church said candidly, "Well, I don't know what kind of problems this person might have had. Maybe it wasn't really the leader's fault" (Interview #78). But persons who experience these dilemmas firsthand are not as likely to dismiss them. These accounts indicate that morally ambivalent behavior by leaders weakens the trust members invest in the charismatic relationship. Perceived violations of this trust are more likely to erode the bonds of commitment and lead to defection.

This chapter began with the idea that some factors or influences play a more critical role in defection because they are sufficient to disrupt normal mechanisms of commitment maintenance and set the disengagement process into motion. Of the factors examined here, four of them are supported by the data: 1) a breakdown in members' insulation from the outside world, 2) unregulated development of dyadic relationships within the communal context, 3) perceived lack of success in achieving world transformation, and 4) inconsistencies between the actions of leaders and the ideals they symbolically represent.

The next chapter looks at some other influences which are identified by defectors as supplemental to the precipitating factors just described. These are basically factors that further impel withdrawal once the disagreement process has been triggered.

CHAPTER FIVE

SOME OTHER FACTORS TO BE CONSIDERED: RELIGION, YOUTH, AND SOCIAL EXPERIMENTATION

An analytical distinction is required here between events or factors which constitute triggering episodes and those which serve as supplemental influences. The latter emerge to provide additional incentives for leaving, once significant disillusionment has set the defection process into motion. Admittedly, such conceptual distinctions are not always empirically clear. Nonetheless, defectors often make these distinctions in their own accounts of why they leave. Examination of these data will, I believe, show that supplementary or secondary factors play an important role in the disengagement sequence.

Religion: The Intrusion of an Alternate Belief System

In some cases, defection may be a result of switching faiths or adopting a different set of beliefs. One factor which four respondents in the sample identified, but which was not specifically hypothesized here, was the direct intrusion of an alternate religious belief system. Such an overt intrusion can, of course, operate as a precipitating factor setting the process of defection into motion (Skonovd, 1981:119). However, it is more common that defectors seek another religious system *after* a major disillusionment or crisis has occurred.

In fact, confrontation with an alternate religious system that is perceived as superior may create the original crisis, explicitly integrated framework from which to critique any other doctrine and organizational structure, and provide a rationale for defecting as well as an alternative paradigm with which to restructure one's life. More typically, however, an individual will encounter dissonance-creating inconsistencies or contradictions within his or her movement's doctrine and/or organizational structure, become generally disaffected after a process of review and reflection, and then encounter an alternative framework which provides both the impetus to defect and the necessary rationale (Skonovd, 1981:119).

Confrontational experiences alone are not good predictors of defection because most or all members of world-transforming movements are confronted with alternate religious belief systems on a regular basis. World-transforming movements are in the business of religious persuasion and, consequently, invite such confrontations as a *routine* part of their recruitment activities. In other words, recruiting and fundraising personnel probably face a steady diet of opposition and challenge from persons of other religious beliefs.

Skonovd argues that defectors typically adopt alternate plausibility structures in the transitional process after their previous commitment has been significantly disrupted. My own data indicate strong support for this hypothesis. Seventy-eight percent of the defectors in this sample report a commitment to another religious group or belief system, and approximately half (53%) identify with conservative fundamentalist/

evangelical or charismatic (neo-Pentecostal) religious groups. This finding will be examined at length in chapter seven. The point here is that these same individuals rarely attribute the *source* of their disillusionment to specific confrontations with alternate religious belief systems. In the transformation sequence, identification with another belief system or organization for most persons comes after major dissonance has set in and the possibilities for leaving become viable. It is in the wake of dissonance that substantial questions and doubts arise about the movement's claims to ultimate truth. At this juncture, alternate religious plausibility structures can provide an explicitly integrated framework from which to dismantle previous beliefs and commitments, and supply a rationale for joining a new group.

The data suggest that members who already register substantial disruption of, or dissatisfaction with, their commitment are more likely to seek out alternatives than those persons whose commitment is intact. Confrontations with representatives of competing movements or perspectives are less likely to sway members who have a strong commitment. Encounters with proselytizers of another faith are quite common in the open marketplace. Though they typically have no immediate effect, these confrontations may later serve as references to fall back on when commitment falters and the individual begins to seriously consider alternative courses of action. Individuals may recall an earlier conversation or encounter with someone of a different religious persuasion to whom they refer in their moments of disillusionment.

The following account by a former Unification Church member is a typical example. After a prolonged separation from the movement raised significant doubts,[1] recollection of earlier encounters with evangelical Christians emerged, leading this individual to explore an alternative belief system.

> A couple of times I had met (evangelical) Christians, too, and they were the only people who could find real holes in the philosophy, point out things that didn't make sense, and that kind of bothered me. The whole thing about Reverend Moon is he supposed to be the Messiah, Christ returned. So somewhere along the line I knew I had to understand who is Christ, who is Jesus Christ and what is the proper understanding and insight as to who he is. People who professed themselves to be Christians, when I talked to them, they had a totally different view and that had me really wondering. After that whole Montreal thing I decided to start checking out the claims of Christ. . . . It is kind of assumed that you're a Christian if you're in the group, but I really didn't know if I was or not. . . . One night I went to see a film, it was kind of a Christian thing, and it blew my mind because it was about the "last days." You know, "Are you a Christian?" "Where are you going?" And it just got me thinking. . . . and I remember praying that night to accept Christ, and I think that was a turning point (Interview #23).

According to an earlier account, the dissonance arising from Gene's protracted separation from the movement introduced the first wave of serious thoughts about leaving. But an alternate religious belief system also played an important part in the process of disengagement. The reason for distinguishing it as a supplemental factor is that it was essentially "put on hold" until after the separation incident took place. That is, the expressed intent to assess evangelical Christian beliefs was not acted upon until after insulating boundaries were disrupted and socialization mechanisms were neutralized or weakened ("After that whole Montreal thing . . .").

Once a disruption in the plausibility structure is introduced, individuals are more willing to reconsider competing claims and beliefs. Previous challenges are more likely to resurface as credible options. In some cases, disillusionment may induce a greater willingness to listen to persons representing other religious beliefs. Alternative views that previously would have been dismissed or ignored are now given a serious ear. Less convinced of one's commitment in the aftermath of a dissonance-creating event, one is simply more vulnerable to dissuasion.

One account by a former member of the Children of God further serves to illustrate this point. Alberto was a full-time member with the movement for almost two years before defecting in September of 1973. He became disillusioned with certain leaders in the movement but was reportedly undecided about whether or not to stay. During a missionary journey in New Mexico, Alberto encountered some Jesus movement people who were critical of Moses David and pointed to numerous shortcomings in the movement's theology. Alberto describes below the impact of this encounter upon his decision to leave.

My doubts came because a rosy picture had always been painted of the Family by the previous shepherds (leaders). They were such nice guys that when something bad happened they would say, "Well, you know, those things happen anywhere," and "Don't let that get you down." But when the new shepherds came in, well, they were bringing in all this bondage to people and condemnation and guilt. That is how the regional shepherds ran their region. So, I said, hey man, this stuff is more widespread, we were told to destroy some of the literature which we had been taught was almost God's word, and I saw contradictions, I saw hypocrisy. Some of the leaders started taking money aside from the literature fund for themselves. They were living high on the hog, whereas the previous leaders didn't. These guys would live above everybody else; they would eat better, they would eat by themselves, maybe they would go out to movies with their wives. Other people in the COG also complained. All this stuff just made me think.

. . . So when I was on the road I ran into some Jesus people that didn't try and lay a trip on me or nothing, but did try to explain to me some of the things in the COG that they thought were wrong. . . . We used to try to stay over with people, a different place every night, and one night we were with these Jesus people in Albuquerque and the leader started talking about Mo, how Mo was trying to get the Koran and the Bible (to harmonize) and he was saying that he thought that was wrong and he didn't, you know, really get all over my case because I was with the COG. He was just trying to show me from the Bible where Mo had gone wrong. So, since he was so nice and everything I thought about that later and I said, "You know, he didn't have that much to gain or lose. You know, maybe what he said was right." And when I came back, I just decided to leave. You know, the Lord was just leading me out, and I left, I made a total break (Interview #34).

According to Alberto, the encounter with Jesus people aided his withdrawal from the Children of God only after contradictions and inconsistencies were realized. Infractions of invested trust by the leadership undermined their moral standing and severely damaged the bond of commitment. In light of this, dissuasion was hastened. The support structure that upheld the posited reality was substantially disrupted and commitment simply became more difficult to maintain for Alberto in the face of perceived "hypocrisy."

A pattern quite similar to the two accounts just described was repeated by a former devotee of the Hare Krishna movement. John was a devotee of the movement for three years prior to leaving in 1971. He joined for "humanitarian" reasons, but became sorely disillusioned when he encountered a former high school friend-turned-"Jesus freak." He credits the contact with this high school friend as crucial in assisting his decision to withdraw.

The first thing I began questioning was the materialism that the leaders of the temple had. You know, the president of the temple had a very nice room, carpeting, a three-sectional couch, very nice furniture, nice things on the wall, a stereo system, the whole bit, all the comforts of home, whereas all the other devotees, had nothing, and that to me was like, you know, where is the sacrifice there?

The other thing which I began seeing as Prabhupada traveled around, he was often in limousines, flew first class, the whole bit, and while he tried to put on the air of being the man who gave up everything, he had anything he wanted, you know. There was no sacrifice there at all.

Well, all this was during the time of the Jesus freak days, and I had a friend in high school who was a Christian and he started coming to me and talking to me-very knowledgeable in the Bible . . . and talking to me about Jesus Christ, presenting me the claims of Jesus Christ. And I knew something of the Bible because I grew up in the Salvation Army, that was my home church as I was growing up, and you can't escape it there. So I knew what he was saying and I began comparing the Bible with the Bhagavad Gita and I was having a lot of questions that couldn't be answered. So that compounded with these other things: the fact that the regular devotees didn't have any possessions hardly, they hardly had any money, they had no beds to sleep on, just mats, four walls to a room, maybe a picture of Krishna on the wall, that kind of thing, whereas the temple president and his assistants had all these nice things. You know, I just couldn't rationalize that any longer. . . .

I was in a park down the block from the temple one afternoon when this friend was speaking with me again and he said, "What are you going to do?" And I said, "There is nothing I can do, I can't fight back anymore." And so we knelt right there in the basketball court and prayed. When I went back to the temple I knew it would be the last time I ever went (Interview #45).

For this ex-devotee, disaffection was already in progress when discussions with a former high school friend began to take place. The disillusionment, precipitated by morally ambivalent actions of movement leaders, was explicitly acknowledged as the "first" evidence of dissonance. Imposition of another belief system—one already known from childhood years—was then said to have a compounding effect, further aiding the individual's decision to disengage from the movement. In this particular instance, another belief system provided an acceptable alternative, which secular life and material values could not. Like the previous accounts, a significant level of dissonance was reportedly experienced here by the individual prior to the contemplation of an alternative perspective.

These three cases illustrate the more typical pattern of the transitional process where an alternate religious belief system is involved. Specifically, a precipitating crisis is likely to occur prior to any serious consideration of other religious faiths. To be sure, defectors who switch faiths usually do not separate these stages in a *theological* sense. Respondents are likely to interpret disruptive occurrences as a direct result of divine intervention on their behalf (e.g., "It was all a part of God's plan"; "the Lord used that to lead me out."). In other words, they are aware of an antecedent fracture of their beliefs or commitment. But such disruptions are usually attributed to hidden supernatural forces. Thus, a prolonged separation from the movement, or the perception of inconsistent and morally ambiguous actions by leaders can be interpreted as a social manifestation of underlying preternatural causes.

Alternative religious belief-systems play a role that may also be fulfilled by other factors that influence the deconversion process in a similar way. These augmentative factors may arise as latently emerging interests or goals, in some cases resulting from maturation through the life cycle.

Youth and Social Experimentation

Though world-transforming movements demand total and uncompromising commitment of core members, there is ample evidence to suggest that many of these involvements are only temporary. They are intense but not enduring. The transitory nature of some communal organizations is well established (Zablocki, 1980; Richardson, et al., 1979). Richardson, et al. (1979:96) refer to a "transition model" to analyze communal movements characterized by patterns of short-term membership. The model is said to identify "a common contemporary tendency for communes to be viewed by members as not necessarily requiring a lifetime commitment."

But experimental or temporary involvements of this nature are not confined to communal groups alone. One observer uses the term "radical departure" to describe youth who join a variety of cultic religious movements and radical political organizations as an effort to establish post-adolescent identity and autonomy (Levine, 1984). Levine argues that once identity crises are resolved many individuals no longer have use for these movements and they return to a more conventional way of life. He says that joiners are often individuals who have been unable to exploit the customary channels of society to gain emotional maturity and psychological independence and opt to use radical groups to solve the dilemmas of growing up. Alienation, loneliness, uncertainty, the search for identity or truth are pervasive features among youth in contemporary culture which make radical departures a commonplace phenomenon.

Since the new religions are almost exclusively *youth* movements, it is important to retain as an analytical frame reference some salient characteristics of youth culture. At least since the 1960s, numerous scholars have described the crystallization of a youth culture that separates the adolescent and youth population from adult roles and institutions (Flacks, 1970; Kenniston, 1971). World-transforming movements tend to recruit their members almost exclusively from among youth who are in transition to adult social and occupational roles (Beckford, 1981; Robbins, 1981). Young persons, it is believed, have fewer responsibilities and obligations, and, consequently, have more expendable time to direct toward social causes or movements. This was especially true of the early 1970s, a period characterized by unprecedented college enrollments, student protest, and exceptional growth of new religious movements (Bromley and Shupe, 1979:94-95; Lofland, 1979:163-64). Modern youth, as a social category, may be understood in terms of their relative freedom from such constraints as domestic commitments, property ownership, and professional investments (Beckford, 1981:4). It would appear that this relative freedom is a necessary condition for modern youth to be regarded as an appropriate target for the new religions (Levine, 1984:28).

Few individuals who join these movements take future conventional interests and responsibilities into account. Settling into a traditional marriage arrangement, rearing children, maintaining ties with their family or orientation and kin, continuing their education, selecting an occupation or career, and gaining employment, or buying a home and durable goods are cultural ideals which are rejected in youthful protest but later appear as acceptable and desirable goals.

These same cultural ideals may serve as latent goals, aiding the disengagement process. When a major crisis or disillusionment experience arises, they act as positive "invitations" for re-entry into mainstream culture. Without a major reason to legitimate or justify leaving, the "invitations" themselves are likely to be seen as "temptations" emanating from satanic spiritual forces or worldly desires that subvert the "truth." Ordinarily, temptations to succumb to Satan or worldliness are dismissed as tests of faith. In many cases, individuals are not likely to admit to having such thoughts and desires because they represent to other members a possible "backsliding" or frailty of conviction. Yet, in the event of a major disruption in one's commitment to a world-transforming movement, these previously rejected or abandoned ideals may be seen in an entirely new light. The sanctions that once prohibited the ideals as morally and spiritually unhealthy lose some of their binding force. Re-entry becomes more attractive and justifiable. Options previously thought to be invalid now gain viability in the eyes of the would-be defector.

One latent or unrecognized concern that repeatedly emerged among defectors during their involvement as members was the increasing awareness of, or concern for, familial and kinship ties outside the movement. Generally, when individuals join a world-transforming movement, they are not keenly aware of the long-range ramifications of severely reduced ties with their families. In the excitement of conversion, individuals tend to be enamored by the discovery of a belief system and support structure that promises to introduce a new age of hope and salvation. Such excitement overshadows any awareness of being isolated from one's family. In fact, movement ideologies stress the importance of familial relations, albeit in a different context (Bromley, et al., 1982; Fichter, 1983; Robbins and Anthony, 1980a). Such efforts can initially serve to arrest apprehensions about possible conflicts in this regard. Often, realization that the situation disallows normal contact and communication with parents, brothers, sisters, grand-parents, etc., will emerge only after considerable time in the movement has elapsed. Once the initial zeal and enthusiasm subsides and the individual's emotional fervor is tempered by the day-to-day realities of living out the religious commitment made, he or she may experience a feeling of loss or regret over the disconnected ties with family and kin. But these feelings and attitudes also exist concomitantly with the individual's sense of dedication and commitment to the movement.

Most likely, such ambivalence does not, by itself, lead to withdrawal. It does, however, create a tension that may lay dormant underneath the committed member's resolve to be a loyal follower. In the event of a major disruption, the subjugation of ties with one's family is more likely to be questioned and critically reexamined. The weakening of the plausibility structure through a triggering event may then act as the impetus toward re-establishing familial ties which, in turn, serves as an emotional and cognitive "bridge" in the transitional process of redefining identity and subjective reality.

The following example illustrates the role of latently valued family ties. When Susan joined the Children of God in October 1974, she was not particularly concerned about the reaction of her parents, nor about the effect her joining might have on their future relationship. The colony she and her husband, Carl, joined was within a few hours drive of her parents' home in Texas and contact did not seem to be an issue. However, after the birth of their son and the couple's subsequent transfer to a colony in another state, these familial ties became more important. Essentially, Susan came to regret the absence of a sustained, affective relationship with her parents. This dilemma was apparently compounded by the perceived forfeiture of the grandparents' relationship to the child.

Following a major disillusioning experience with local colony leadership Susan acknowledges, retrospectively, that the prospect of leaving was enhanced by the fact that she could spend more time with her parents and they, in turn, could now "enjoy their grandbaby."

RESPONDENT: I didn't think about it much at the time, but I know when I joined my daddy was hurt, he was let down, because all his life he thought, ideally, you know, everybody had to get married and have a home (house) and a car, and all that. And here Carl and I got married and had a baby and we were off in this group, so I would say he was disappointed. . . . When we were in the Austin colony, we were still pretty close by—my folks lived in San Antonio—so I could call them or write them, they even came up to visit us a couple of times. But when we moved to Oklahoma City it was totally different up there. I hardly ever wrote them there.

INTERVIEWER: Why?

RESPONDENT: Well, basically, I was pressured under such a schedule, you know; I had so much to do that I didn't have time hardly to ever read my Bible. And, of course, phone calls were out because they were just too expensive, so they wouldn't let us do that. So, basically, I didn't write to my folks because of my schedule, I was so pressured.

INTERVIEWER: Did that bother you?

RESPONDENT: Yes. I remember I wanted to go home for Christmas really bad, and they told me I could probably go to see my folks, you know, because I hadn't seen them in about six or eight months and they had not seen the baby in a long time and this was their first grandbaby and they really wanted to see him. So they said, "You can go down this Christmas," you know, and they were kind of questioning me like, "Do you think it will be profitable?" And I said, "What do you mean will it be profitable?" And they said, "Well, you know, would they really be able to give you clothes and things?" And I said, "Well, they will give me a little bit of stuff, you know." Finally, about a few days before Christmas they told me I couldn't go. So I was really hurt because I had planned on it, I had counted on it.

. . . I think one good thing was, after we decided to leave when we were in Wichita Falls, I kind of looked forward to spending some time with my folks and letting them enjoy their grandbaby. Before the baby was born, when it was just Carl and myself, it wasn't that big of a deal. But the baby made a big difference. You know what I mean? (Interview #14).

The observed contradiction between the movement's claim to be a "Family" and the colony leadership's insistence on exposing the couple's sick child to inclement weather was especially significant in light of the emerging concern for familial ties. This invalidating experience essentially caused them to withdraw emotionally from the group. It served to push them toward a defensive stance and forced them to contract psychologically, realigning primary loyalties along family lines. In this realignment of loyalties, the reconciliation of disconnected ties with kin outside the movement (i.e., Susan's parents) became increasingly desirable.

Another case involving family ties was described by a young woman who left the Hare Krishna movement. Kathleen was a devotee for six months before defecting in May of 1980. Her doubts were reportedly created by the controversial practice of "transcendental trickery." But, as remarks from the following dialogue suggest, she was also significantly influenced by her parents' attitudes and reactions.

RESPONDENT: I didn't tell my parents until after I was living there a week or two.

Then my mother got frenetic and worried, and consulted some people and then read all sorts of articles and got really scared to death.

. . . I talked to [the leaders] about my parents being really upset about this whole thing. They had suggested that my parents were misdirected and caught up in the material world, and all that. It wasn't any sort of big thing where they gave a lecture about it or anything. But once I told them how upset my parents were they did suggest that it was not good to associate with them right then.

INTERVIEWER: How did you feel about that?

RESPONDENT: Well, I didn't feel that it was such a good answer. That was another thing that disturbed me. Because I felt that the people in the temple were not really much better off than people outside of the temple. While some people may be on a spiritual path . . . that doesn't mean they're any less materialistic, you know. It's just a process. So, that was one of the things that kind of made me a little edgy. . . .

INTERVIEWER: You mentioned earlier that transcendental trickery was the thing that really created a lot of doubt and dissatisfaction. How about your relationship to your parents? Would you say that was a factor involved in your decision to leave?

RESPONDENT: Yes, I think so. There was a lot of pressure from my parents. I felt a great sense of guilt because my mother was really climbing the walls (Interview #37).

When Kathleen joined the movement she was 19 years old, self-supporting and living away from home. But she admitted to being "very close" to her parents prior to conversion. A strong negative reaction by her mother seemed to feed apprehensions about the organization. When asked how she felt about the leadership's recommendation to dissociate from her parents during the novitiate stage, she replied, ". . . that was one of the things that kind of made me a little edgy." It is evident by Kathleen's continued involvement that she suppressed these apprehensions at least for a short time. But the concerns later re-emerged to aid her decision to quit the movement. Like the previous case, the pull of family ties played a key part in the disengagement dynamics.

Parents and families can exert a qualified influence on a convert's choice to leave. While the influence of families seemingly never are identified by defectors as triggering disillusionment they are frequently mentioned as contributing in other ways. For example, Susan and Kathleen both allude to close family ties and parental reactions towards joining. Given the centrality of the family as a primary socialization agent, it is worth asking if there is a correlation between family affinity and disaffiliation. The measures of family influence used in the study permit us to explore three explicit questions: 1) Does prior closeness to one's family of orientation affect the likelihood of disaffiliation? 2) Does a positive adolescent experience with one's family of orientation affect the likelihood of disaffiliation? 3) Do parental reactions or attitudes toward joining affect the likelihood of disaffiliation?[2] The responses to these questions were tabulated and analyzed in contingency tables shown in Table 5.1.

Table 5.1 FAMILY VARIABLES BY MEMBERSHIP STATUS

	Defectors %	Defectors (N)	Members %	Members (N)
A. *Parental Attitudes*				
Favorable	21.05	(4)	78.95	(15)
Unfavorable	57.75	(41)	42.25	(30)
$x^2 = 8.07$, $p = .005$				
B. *Adolescent Experience*				
Smooth	62.79	(27)	37.21	(16)
Not smooth	38.30	(18)	61.70	(29)
$x^2 = 5.39$, $p = .020$				
C. *Prior Family Closeness*				
Close	54.90	(28)	45.10	(23)
Not close	43.59	(17)	54.41	(22)
$x^2 = 1.13$, $p = .288$				

Table 5.2 FAMILY CLOSENESS BY MEMBERSHIP STATUS CONTROLLING FOR ADOLESCENT EXPERIENCE

	Defectors %	Defectors (N)	Members %	Members (N)
Smooth				
Close	60.00	(21)	40.00	(14)
Not close	75.00	(6)	25.00	(2)
Not smooth				
Close	43.75	(7)	56.25	(9)
Not close	35.48	(11)	64.52	(20)

The findings indicate that parental and familial influences may indeed help to explain why youth leave. It was found that both parental disapproval and a smooth adolescent experience with one's family were related significantly to disaffiliation, while prior closeness to family was independent (Table 5.1). It was only slightly more likely that defectors reported family closeness before entry, but the difference was not statistically significant. However, those who reported a smooth adolescent experience with their family were more likely to defect. The same finding holds for those who experienced parental objections to joining. Although the majority of respondents perceived parental attitudes as unfavorable, it was much more likely for those whose parents were favorable to remain members than to leave.

To examine the interrelationship between family variables several other contingency tables were analyzed. Here it was found that prior closeness to family was related to adolescence in that those whose adolescent experience with family was smooth were more likely to be close to their family (81%). When examined as a trivariate relationship in table 5.2, holding constant adolescent experience, there appears to be a small relationship between family closeness and defector status. As might be expected, the majority of those respondents with smooth adolescence had close family ties and were more likely to disaffiliate whereas most of those whose adolescence was not smooth were not close to their families and they remained in the movement. It would appear to be the interaction of adolescent experience and family closeness which explains defection and indeed a more rigorous statistical analysis of these data support this conclusion.[3]

A critical finding is shown in Table 5.3 which demonstrates an association between family closeness and parental attitudes. In families which were close and more likely to have an unfavorable attitude towards the child joining, the respondents were more likely to withdraw (70%). On the other hand, those whose parents were favorable were more likely to remain members (86%). Yet, if families were not close, parental attitudes were unrelated to staying or leaving. A pattern quite similar to this is shown for respondents when the measure of adolescent experience with family is substituted for family closeness in Table 5.4.

Table 5.3. PARENTAL ATTITUDES BY MEMBERSHIP STATUS CONTROLLING FOR FAMILY CLOSENESS

	Defectors		Members	
	%	(N)	%	(N)
Close				
Favorable	14.29	(2)	85.71	(12)
Unfavorable	70.27	(26)	29.73	(11)
Not Close				
Favorable	40.00	(2)	60.00	(3)
Unfavorable	44.12	(15)	35.88	(19)

Table 5.4. PARENTAL ATTITUDES BY MEMBERSHIP STATUS CONTROLLING FOR ADOLESCENT EXPERIENCE

	Defectors		Members	
	%	(N)	%	(N)
Smooth				
Favorable	25.00	(3)	75.00	(9)
Unfavorable	77.42	(24)	22.58	(7)
Not smooth				
Favorable	25.00	(1)	75.00	(6)
Unfavorable	42.50	(17)	57.50	(23)

The results here complement impressions gleaned from the interviews and suggest that parental and familial influences have provisional affects. The measures of family influence denote key interactions which shed light on the likelihood of staying or leaving. With reference to leaving, parental disapproval was salient particularly among youth who reported a smooth adolescent experience and to a lesser extent a closeness to family before joining. Thus, there is some evidence that the formation of a healthy and harmonious family bond during the critical years of adolescence and young adulthood, while not preventing affiliation, may help to promote disaffiliation. But the impact should be qualified as an augmentative one; that is, not a precipitating affect.

Conversely, favorable parental attitudes towards joining were related to remaining in the movement among converts who reported a closeness to family prior to entry. Stayers were four times more likely than leavers to report parental approval. A similar correlation was shown among stayers whose parents approved. Therefore, it seems apparent that the direction or outcome of the cult career, whether the individual chooses to stay or leave, is to some degree influenced by one's parents and the quality of life in the years preceding conversion.

The estimated weight of family influences among defectors varied. Some mentioned them only briefly while others were more conscious of their effects. Those who were careful to articulate familial concerns tended to emphasize the importance of letting the individual make his or her own decision about leaving. Patience, trust and unconditional love were parental qualities described by these youth as most critical. On the other hand, research reveals that increased alienation between parents and children often is attributed to a lack of trust and a related "fear of deprogramming" (Ungerleider and Wellisch, 1983:209). Joining a world-transforming movement may temporarily threaten familial ties, placing them in a tenuous relationship when parents and kin disapprove. But when an individual becomes disillusioned and begins to reevaluate his or her direction of life, this may lead to support from one's family to disaffiliate.

Though parental disapproval appears to have a significant impact—at least when adolescent socialization experiences and preconversion bonds are strong—it should not be equated with extreme parental reactions. In a few cases, an overly negative reaction by parents only created anger, resentment, and even bitterness over a son or daughter's decision to join. Both defectors and members expressed a strong aversion to parental responses which involved shouting and anger. These were said to be ineffective and even counterproductive. An illustration of this can be seen in the remarks of a member of the Hare Krishna movement.

My dad blew up when I joined the temple. He said I was crazy and that I was throwing away my whole future and all that. . . . But all he's got to show for his troubles is two heart attacks and a mountain of debts. So who wants to be like him? . . . When I'm around him it only confirms what I've decided to do here (Interview #62).

These findings support an earlier study by Beckford (1982). Beckford examined parental attitudes toward family members joining the Unification Church in Great Britain and found that responses of anger often backfired leading to a "vicious spiral" of heated accusations between parents and converts. Angry responses only increased the deterioration of the relationship. Among my respondents, reports of hostile parental reactions were sparse. Most described their parents' attitudes as "worried" or "upset." Beckford also found a minority of angry responses by parents of converts. He notes that "the majority were more anxious about preserving the moral basis of trust in which a continuing and future relationship could be grounded" (Beckford, 1982:50).

Latent concerns are not limited solely to families. Changes may take place involving modified outlooks toward one's education. Converts are typically of college age and join before completing a degree. Data for this study indicate that 56 percent of the sample joined before completing a degree, while only 16 percent finished college. Thus, members who do not complete a college education may later experience reservations about such a choice. Education is an asset that can be utilized in any situation and some individuals may become apprehensive about having lost the opportunity entirely. Consequently, the thought of going back to school can become inviting for those who have had some time to reflect. However, committed members also know that it may conflict with collective goals of the organization. They know that the movement cannot possibly realize its goals if adherents have divided interests and only part-time commitments. Therefore, latent interests may be suppressed or ignored. If they *are* verbalized, other members may discourage the individual from entertaining these ideas. The individual most likely will be reminded that "true" knowledge is found exclusively in the group's message, or in the words of the prophet-founder.

Moreover, pursuing a course of action such as returning to school lacks adequate legitimation on its own grounds. If socialization mechanisms have been effective, it is not reason enough, by itself, to justify leaving the movement. It is here that the triggering episode is so important. A disillusioning event can effectively disrupt the plausibility structure of the group and provide legitimate grounds for realizing latent educational aspirations.

Such was the case for one former Unification Church member. Andrea was a member of the church for three years before leaving in March, 1978. After approximately two and a half years involvement with the movement, she reportedly purchased some books while preparing for a church-sponsored conference in San Francisco and read them during her free time. Andrea found the experience enlightening and afterward discovered a growing desire to spend time alone reading. Subsequently, she expressed a wish to return to school. However, she did not act upon these quiescent interests until after having a disturbing encounter with a superior. Her story is described in the following account.

> While I was in San Francisco working for the science conference, I had bought two books and I just started to read them a lot. I guess I just found that being able to read again was really good for me. . . . I was finding that it was more and more important to me to have time to spend by myself and time to read. I thought a lot about going back to school. . . .

> Well, I was having some conflict with someone I was working with on the staff who was in a position over me. One day we were arguing about selling newspapers and I said, "I wish that you would try to see it from my point of view." And he just pounded his fist on my desk and said, "you are not supposed to have a point of view"; meaning that since I was in the 'Cain' position and he was in the 'Abel' position, I was not supposed to have a point of view, and he walked out. And it was on that day that I just really got angry and decided that I would make the decisions in my life, I would decide where I went to school, and I would decide when I would go back, and I would decide when I would go home for my brother's wedding, and how long I would stay, and a lot of other things that they had been trying to control. . . .

> So in March of 1978, I wrote a long letter to my immediate central figure and I said that I wanted to go back to school. He suggested that I wait a couple of weeks until the next higher central figure came back from Europe, and when he did I went to speak to him. I was told if I went back to school as a full-time student I wouldn't be allowed to live in the World Missions Center. I would have to live on my own in New York City. I didn't want to do that so I went back to school in Michigan (Interview #15).

These remarks indicate that the surfacing of latent goals regarding school were a catapulting force toward disaffiliation when coupled with a disturbing incident with a

64

staff leader. It seems reasonable to assume that the dissatisfaction she reportedly experienced before the confrontation may have been resolved by finding a means of channeling this frustration constructively within the movement. For example, some members of the Unification Church who show intellectual promise are sent to the church's seminary in Barrytown, New York. It is not inevitable, by any means, that Andrea's dissatisfaction about school should have led to her departure from the church.

All successful social movements must be able to channel and redirect frustrations, turning them into productive energies that build and strengthen commitment. World-transforming movements create highly controlled social environments that are conducive to recognizing disgruntled members and reconciling them to the group. In this case, it may be that the timing of the triggering episode is especially significant. It is worth noting that the encounter occurs before a resolution of latent interests can be identified and achieved. If the problem was identified sooner, it is quite possible that the group might have negotiated a solution to Andrea's dilemma. Movement leadership may have suggested that Andrea be transferred to a C.A.R.P. team (Collegiate Association for the Research of Principles) where she could have been near a university and taken courses. Or, perhaps Andrea could have been persuaded to delay returning to school while given an assignment that would permit more reading time. However, the problem was not resolved when the crisis event took place, and the latent interests which had already surfaced only supplied additional incentives to leave.

Pat, also a former member of the Unification Church, is another example of a person wanting to return to school. He was a full-time member for fifteen months before defecting in 1979. He reportedly grew disenchanted and impatient with a stagnated situation. Out of feelings of impatience and frustration, Pat decided to go back to college. He gives a brief account of how this developed.

> You would have to understand the situation I was in. It was like I was in a rut, everybody was in a rut because we weren't doing anything but working our asses off in this restaurant that Moon owned on the coast. We were just busboys, that's it. And the church was happy because we were making money. That's all they were concerned about.

> . . . After awhile it really started to get to me and everything, I was very depressed, and I'd been thinking a lot about going back to school in Virginia. So I wrestled with that for about a month and then I decided that, you know, that's what I had to do. And I told my superior that I was leaving, and he tried his best to talk me out of it. He said, "Give it some more time and we can work it out." And he was a good guy and all, it wasn't his fault. We had a pretty good relationship, but I knew I had to get out of there (Interview #16).

The prospect of resuming an education provided a concrete solution to Pat's dilemma. Since he had come to identify himself as merely a "busboy" engaged in wasted activities, the idea of returning to college furnished a powerful rationale. Members gravitating toward departure often begin to search for legitimate reasons to further empower the chosen course of defection and surmount the obstacles deployed by the movement to deter them. In Pat's case, it is not clear whether returning to school was a *post facto* justification or a pre-existing concern. But focusing on this short-range goal appears to be a helpful step in the disengagement process.

The almost exclusive reliance upon young adults in world-transforming movements has its advantages and disadvantages. These movements have unquestionably benefitted from the zeal of youth who, as a unique social category, have the expendable time and freedom to make total commitments. However, the distinct disadvantage that these movements face is that they must strive to maintain commitment among persons who are in transition to adult roles and identities. As converts explore human relationships and carve out meaning in their lives, they are also apt to change directions. Youthful members may change their minds about what they want out of life after a year or two of involvement. Thus, simply due to the nature of the age group they have targeted for recruitment, the movements face the continual problem of defection. Intensive socialization processes are designed to prevent extraneous goals or interests from arising. Nonetheless, latent concerns such as recapturing family ties or returning to college are potential threats that will arise.

I have chosen to classify these factors as supplementary because, by themselves, they are rarely seen as valid reasons to defect. They are more likely to reinforce withdrawal once or triggering episode has occurred. In the absence of precipitating factors, they are likely to be viewed as illegitimate concerns influenced by selfish motives or evil forces. Committed members will find it extremely difficult to leave merely because they want to settle into a traditional marriage arrangement, maintain ties with their family of orientation or continue their education. However, as augmentative influences, they supply a critical boost to the reticent defector. One can resurrect the previously discounted "temptations" and redefine them in the light of an invalidating experience, consider them in combination, and decide that one's family or education are valid concerns after all. Taking into consideration the life-cycle stage of most converts, it is with good reason that world-transforming movements lose many adherents as they grow older and discover shifting ambitions, interests and needs.

CHAPTER SIX
TACTICAL MODES OF EXIT

Our attention now shifts to the programmatics of leave-taking. Can we assume that leavers give much systematic thought to how they will defect? In other words, do they develop plans and tactical modes of departure? There is by no means a consensus among the few studies that have addressed this topic. Skonovd (1981) introduced the phrase, "strategies of leave-taking" to indicate that such planning is present in the actions of defectors. Yet, Skonovd's study does not reveal much diversity in exiting modes. He finds that an overwhelming majority leave stealthily and that a "public leave taking is extremely difficult, if not impossible, for most" (Skonovd, 1981:122). Recently, Beckford (1985) has asserted that strategies of departure are uncharacteristic of leavers. In a study of ex-Unification Church members, he found a common theme: "nobody made plans for leaving" (Beckford, 1985:159). "[T]he decision to leave," says Beckford (1985:159), "was usually taken on the spur of the moment and was not followed by any careful planning for the move."

Several questions are raised by these studies. First, do leavers develop planned departures? Second, if so, do most defectors leave stealthily, and how accurately does previous research describe the full range of voluntary exiting modes? Third, if strategies of leave-taking are characterized by greater diversity, are there any factors which might help to explain the selection of different modes?

Among the individuals I interviewed, three patterns or strategies of leave-taking emerged: covert, overt, and declarative. The internal logic and particular advantages of selected exiting modes are the focus of this chapter.

The Covert Departure

Often individuals preparing to defect choose to leave in a covert manner. Forty-two percent of the defectors in this sample left covertly. Persons who pursue such a mode of departure generally feel that the act of leaving should be done secretly, without drawing attention to oneself. They refrain from telling others because of the possible complications that could arise if the defector's plans were "leaked" to the group. Because of the powerful influence the group exerts over its members, defecting individuals want to avoid discussing or debating the decision. Making intentions known invites the possibility of being talked out of leaving. Since detachment and disengagement are always difficult, covert withdrawal avoids unwelcome emotional turmoil and conflict.

Covert departures typically involve exits during the night when others are sleeping, or during a normal routine of daily activities in which departure corresponds to a time in which the individual is more or less alone. The latter can be done without generating unnecessary questions or suspicion. For example, an individual may wait until he or she is out fundraising and simply leave when others are not around. Or, in some cases, where insulating boundaries are disrupted, individuals already separated from the movement may find that the best strategy for leave-taking is a quiet but permanent disappearance. Seven of the eight defectors who experienced prolonged separation from the movement were of this type. Only one returned to the group before deciding to leave permanently. This type of strategy suggests that the exit is made during a time in which the individual will meet the least resistance.

For covert defectors, to announce or even deliberate one's intentions of leaving in front of the group is seen as jeopardizing the act. Once the decision is made, the individual endeavors to keep it a secret, thereby cognitively safeguarding the plan from any attempted refutation. Confiding in a close friend may even be discounted for fear that the conversation will be overheard and leaked back to leaders. Exposed intentions of defecting run a greater risk of a possible renegotiation of social reality by others, particularly leaders. The defecting person may still feel partly influenced by, or subject to, the demands of the leadership. The felt obligations that accompany entrenched patterns of leader-follower interaction do not dissipate overnight. Consequently, avoidance of a confrontation with movement leaders is highly desired.

A typical example of covert departure was illustrated in the following case. Jim, a former member of the Unification Church, described leaving the movement while in California. He had mixed feelings about defecting because of admittedly strong attachments to the people and the ideals in the community. He resolved this dissonance by choosing to leave in the middle of the night, thereby avoiding confrontations that might deter him from his plan of action. Jim gave the following account of his departure:

> My doubts just grew and grew until I could think of nothing else but to leave; to leave, that was the only thing that was on my mind. But at the same time, I didn't see how I could leave; I felt like I was really attached to the people that were there.

> But this one day the only thing I could think of was to plan how I was going to leave. And that night came and I knew I was just going to get up in the middle of the night and gather everything I had and walk out of that camp, and basically that's what happened. I got up and I knew exactly where everybody was, I put my backpack on, I put everything I had on and walked straight out of that camp in the middle of the night. I encountered one brother at the gate as I was going out and I just turned to him and I said, "Don't try to stop me," and I just kept walking (Interview #4).

For Jim, this surreptitious exit helped to minimize much of the interference that would have otherwise accompanied an open departure. By leaving during the night, he simply reduced the number of potential obstacles that could have made the act more unpleasant. A covert mode of exit helped to eliminate added confusion, making the departure as simple and expeditious as possible. Dissonant information may have threatened the rationale for defection. Thus, to assure the defector of a consistent and undisturbed line of thinking and acting, the departure was made in secret.

Covert departure also helps the defecting individual to "save face" or avoid a possibly embarrassing encounter. Other members may feel the defector is a deserter to the cause, thus employing verbal and nonverbal sanctions in order to convey the group's displeasure at the individual's decision to leave. Moreover, the defector may not want to be reminded of purported repercussions that are sometimes said to befall those who leave. Reports of forewarned repercussions are quite common, and typically single out the apostate as a discreditable turncoat. The following comments by one defector are an example of this:

> It was pretty unnerving actually. They make you feel like you're running out on the Messiah. It's like what Judas did to Jesus, you know. God was going to turn his back on you; foresake you and everything (Interview #20).

Individuals who choose a covert departure are more than likely responding to strong attachments and beliefs from which they still are not completely free. An alternate perspective may not have congealed and thus, the individual is between social worlds. Covert withdrawal helps to prevent old influences from impeding the transition to an alternate plausibility structure. Again, Jim's remarks about covert withdrawal suggest this to be the case.

> I wasn't really sure I was doing the right thing, mind you. They had something there that was different from anything I'd ever experienced. . . . I accepted that they were more spiritually mature and that they could communicate with God. . . . [But] I was bothered that they would never allow me access to materials outside of the community. . . . For awhile I was convinced by the fact that they said, "Well, you're so spiritually immature you'll be swayed by the devil, by Satan. . . . [But] when the doubt started coming, well, I think I just had to be off by myself to really think through it all, and I didn't want ten people around me while I was doing it.

Accounts by covert defectors show a greater penchant for avoiding dissonance produced by internalized beliefs and group pressures. In other words, these individuals express a greater unwillingness and/or inability to cope with the dissonance associated with leaving. This appears to relate to the difficulty which such individuals have in detaching themselves from the old plausibility structure. Remarks by two covert defectors are cases in point.

> A lot of things go through your mind. You hear stories about people who leave, how miserable they are because they are not serving God. I remember they (Children of God) used to use that Scripture that said, "a dog returns to his vomit." Have you ever heard that? That's how they would describe someone who left (Interview #1).

> It was taught that if you left the church you would lose your salvation, you would be spiritually dead. . . . I remember the feeling I had when I would find out somebody left. It was like mourning for the loss of a soul. It was very difficult to ever think about leaving (Interview #19).

Being "spiritually dead" or "miserable" are expectations about apostasy which are learned in the group. These expectations are part of the socialization process that is designed to distinguish and polarize the moral certainty of the movement and the corrupted world outside. A "dog" who "returns to his vomit" is a graphic metaphorical statement taken from the Bible (II Peter 2:22) condemning the apostate. Essentially, the group is claiming the ontological status therein. Such tactics of constructing absolute standards of right and wrong are intended to inhibit backsliding. For covert defectors, the tactics designed to stigmatize the apostate appear to be effective to the degree that these individuals seek to circumvent an open confrontation with the group.

The Overt Departure

The overt mode of withdrawal is one which is done without fanfare or public "announcements"' to the group. Individuals who choose this form typically leave quietly, though not secretively. The decision is usually acted upon after deliberation with a leader or leaders. After attempts at resolution fail, the individual is reluctantly permitted to leave. It should be distinguished from the declarative mode which involves a strategy of making an open announcement or declaration to the group that one is leaving. The latter is typically a sudden or abrupt act performed with marked deliberateness and even anger, while the overt mode is less demonstrative and less agitated. Overt exits were found to be the most common of the three types (47% of defectors).

In this mode, dissatisfactions are openly expressed and conveyed by the individual to the leadership. In turn, efforts usually are made by the leadership to counsel the disenchanted individual to remain. However, in some cases, individuals may be forced to make a choice to either abide by certain organizational requisites or leave.[1] Some attempts may be made to resolve the problem by transferring the member to another location or assigning him/her to another job. In effect, several attempts are likely to be made to work through the crisis. However, when these attempts fail to resolve the problem or renew the individual's commitment, the person in question reluctantly may be allowed to leave. Unlike the covert mode, overt departure involves a situation in which the leadership is aware of the individual's desire or intention to leave.

Overt withdrawal seems to find some justification in the fact that the individual sincerely endeavors to settle the conflict by counseling with leaders or other select members. Legitimation takes the form of the statement, "Well, at least I tried." The defector may attempt to reason with the leadership, to suggest a compromise or a modification of existing rules or expectations. But when a compromise or agreement cannot be reached, the individual is able to use the impasse as a further step in the legitimation sequence catapulting one toward the act of disaffiliation.

An example cited earlier of a young woman in the Unification Church who sought to return to school is an excellent illustration of this type.[2] Following a disturbing encounter with a leader and the emergence of latent goals regarding school, this woman approached the leadership openly with her dissatisfaction. She requested that she be allowed to return to school as a full-time student while remaining in the church. But the leadership refused to compromise to that extent and forced her to make a choice between school or the group. If she returned to college, Andrea was told, she wouldn't be allowed to live in the center. "I didn't want to do that," she states, "so I went back to school in Michigan" (Interview #15).

The data also show that overt defectors are more likely than covert defectors to have acute conflicts over explicit policy-related issues. For example, the case just noted centers largely around a policy regarding school. Here I want to suggest that the mode of exit selected is associated with the type of problem perceived by the defector. While covert defectors tend more to struggle with vague, unfocused discontents or deep emotional attachments, overt and declarative defectors are more likely to have problems with specific policies, thus dictating a more confrontive approach to conflict resolution through negotiation or open vocalization of grievances.[3]

Different strategies of leave-taking correspond to certain types of rationales that are also a result of the amount of time one has spent in the movement. Apparently, veteran members are more likely than novices to confront the organization and voice their dissatisfactions over policies and practices.[4] On the other hand, novices are more likely to avoid confrontations by exiting furtively. Table 6.1 reveals a significant relationship between the length of membership and the selected mode of exit. Twelve of 13 (92%) defectors with less than one year of involvement left the movement in a covert manner. In effect, short-term members had a near monopoly on covert departures. Conversely, 25 of 32 (78%) defectors with one year or more of membership left their respective movements in either an overt or declarative mode. More experienced members preferred to "get things out in the open" or "lay their cards on the table." Unlike newer members, they felt their tenures entitled them to make demands or to press for explanations. In essence, these liberties shaped both the strategies and rationales of exiting among seasoned members.

Table 6.1. **SELECTED STRATEGIES OF LEAVE-TAKING BY LENGTH OF MEMBERSHIP**

Length of Membership	Covert %	(N)	Overt/Declarative %	(N)	Total %	(N)
Less than 1 year	92	(12)	8	(1)	100	(13)
1-3 years	22	(4)	78	(14)	100	(18)
More than 3 years	21	(3)	79	(11)	100	(14)

$x^2 = 18.77$
$df = 2$
p .01

Comments by an ex-member of the Hare Krishna movement further illustrate the relationship between the overt mode of exit and policy-related conflicts. This particular young man became upset over methods of fundraising practiced by the movement. He approached the leadership with his grievances in an effort to effect some policy changes, but was unsuccessful. Although previously he was entertaining the idea of leaving, the meeting with the leadership was said to help make his decision easier.

> They said that because the ultimate purpose we were working for was transcendent to any earthly morality, that it didn't matter if we lied in order to raise money. But I knew that was wrong and I told them so. You know, they always got so angry when the media would tell lies about the movement, and yet we were just as bad. But they couldn't see it. . . . So I think that just made it easier for me to make up my mind [to leave] (Interview #33).

These remarks indicate the individual's sincerity in reaching a solution openly. They further suggest that the devotee would not have been comfortable with the idea of a covert departure. But, his unsuccessful effort to convince the leadership of a different approach to fundraising became an additional reason to see continuation as undesirable. It augments, rather than threatens, the rationale for leave-taking.

In another case, also cited earlier, the conflict involved a policy of marriage and celibacy. Bill and Denise left the Unification Church primarily because Bill became unwilling to remain separated from his wife. Bill grew very doubtful that their marriage would ever be "blessed" by Reverend Moon and persuaded Denise to leave with him. Rather than leave by the back door, however, they chose to meet with the leadership before finally departing. Bill describes the meeting in the following account:

> I think I had to go through that or I never would have been able to understand what I understand now, okay? It was necessary. They had to understand where I was coming from and that I just could not function in that situation any more. . . . At first, they tried to talk me out of it, but at the end of that meeting I'd say they finally saw my point of view. I wasn't going to be much help to them in my frame of mind, and they knew it. I didn't want to be there any longer. I wasn't happy . . . and other people were going to see that, and that wasn't going to help anyone. So they said, "Okay, you can leave" (Interview #25).

Persons who leave in an overt mode are more likely to feel they have either 1) some recourse to amending grievances, or 2) justifiable grounds to leave based on unreasonable or overly rigid policies. Both situations call for some form of disclosure and interchange between members and leaders. The second reason identified here is especially applicable to cases involving a "declarative" mode of exit.

The Declarative Departure

Upon making a decision to leave, some individuals feel a need to declare intentions and state openly reasons for defecting. This kind of strategy serves to settle the issue of disaffiliation clearly and decisively. While it is usually a culmination of ideas and doubts pondered by the would-be defector for weeks or months, the act itself is carried out in haste. Approximately 11 percent of defectors fall into this category.

The declarative mode is typically non-negotiable. The defector who finally decides to leave in this manner is simply unwilling to consider alternative possibilities or suggestions offered by the group. The individual has made up his/her mind and will not be restrained or dissuaded from the chosen course of action. The defector will most likely give a brief explanation of the rationale for leave-taking, state it emphatically and with a tone of finality, and then depart. In some cases, it is analogous to a marital partner announcing to one's spouse that the marriage has failed and that he or she is walking out. The decision is said to be firm and the defector moves in a swift and unwavering fashion to complete the act. The religious group, like the unsuspecting husband or wife, is caught off guard and is less able to mobilize defenses to stop the determined recreant.

The following case is an example of a declarative mode of departure. Carol, a former member of the Unification Church, left in part because of a policy which allowed only men to occupy positions of leadership. She decided to leave after experiencing intense frustration with the leadership's purportedly "chauvinistic" attitudes toward women. Her discouragement and frustration were apparently vented to others at the center when she openly announced her plans to leave.

When I first left, I just bolted (out). It was the only way that I could really get enough steam up. It was like—I would have to say that I didn't have the courage to just go out and close the door. I had to, you know, just go crashing out, all pissed off and [yelling that] this happened and that happened. So when I left I was full of a lot of anger. But I think that was the only way I could get up the momentum to move, you know, which I consider a shortcoming on my part. I would much rather have just been able to calmly go away from the situation. But, nonetheless, I went away all pissed off (Interview #30).

The strategy of a declarative mode is utilized when doubt, grievances, and frustrations have proved to be insurmountable. It is typically a release of bottled-up sentiments that have not been shared or resolved. Again, to use the analogy of a failed marriage, declarative departure is akin to a situation in which the spouse is unable to admit to or express his or her growing disaffection. Research on divorce shows that spouses may begin to disengage emotionally long before verbalization of the fact (Federico, 1979:94-5). "As with other significant life decisions," Federico (1979:94) argues, "it (separation or divorce) may be reached silently and after a period of 'backburner' mental activity." Though the decision may appear in conscious thought, "it is likely to be rapidly suppressed because its implications are threatening" (Federico, 1979:94). Thus, by the time one's grievances are voiced, it is often too late. The decision to separate or dissolve the relationship has already been made. Verbalization, at this point, is merely an announcement.

What may appear to be an irrational or impulsive act to others actually can be understood as a subtle psychological maneuver intended to intimidate the opposition. Weiss (1975:25) refers to intimidation as a "weapon" brandished by disaffected spouses in the throes of marital disengagement. Intimidating one's detractors immobilizes them and allows the aspiring apostate or divorcé(e) a brief forum to inventory perceived wrong doings and infidelities. Where the strain of silence or a deaf ear has only increased estrangement, the individual may feel compelled to lash out at the other(s), inflicting guilt and assessing blame. Such displays of emotion may also signal anxieties and trepidations about separation, referred to by Weiss (1979:40) as "separation distress." Symptoms of separation distress include apprehensiveness, anxiety, fear and even panic (Weiss 1976:49). One may speculate, then, that the declarative act has an advantageous interactional affect in helping to relieve tensions surrounding departure as well as allaying concerted efforts of deterrence.

Exiting modes entail different ploys and carry certain advantages. Each is marked by its own internal logic and is tied to the constellation of personal and social factors wherein one finds himself of herself. In particular, one's length of membership exhibits a significant influence. We can generalize the observed patterns of leave-taking by saying that covert defectors tend to be novices who demonstrate a tendency to wrestle with vague, unfocused discontents or deep emotional attachments which may be difficult for them to manage or articulate in an open confrontation with leaders. These individuals express a greater inability to cope with dissonance that accompanies an overt mode of exit and, consequently, they choose to leave by the back door. Overt defectors are more likely to be seasoned members who become involved in conflicts over explicit policy-related issues which prompt a direct approach to conflict-resolution through open confrontation or negotiation. Declarative defectors are veterans who confront, but do not wish to negotiate. There is no longer anything they wish to gain. While they may be said to share some similarities with covert defectors by virtue of a prolonged silence or inability to express growing frustrations, they clearly may be distinguished by their methods of ultimate resolution.

In the next chapter, I want to look at the final stage of defection. This involves the defector's acquisition of a new identity, lifestyle, and worldview. It will attempt to answer questions such as, "Where do ex-members go after they leave?" What is the readjustment process like? What kinds of lifestyles do they lead and where do they fit in? These are important questions that should help inform our understanding of how the process of defection is completed.

PART THREE
SOCIAL RELOCATION

CHAPTER SEVEN

RE-ENTRY AND REINTEGRATION

It should be recognized that defection is not merely a process of detachment, but also a process of reformulation and selection of an alternate identity and worldview. A transition of this nature necessarily implies a destination. By destination, I mean a distinctively different perspective and support structure which enables the individual to make the adjustment to a new life. Adoption of a new plausibility structure helps to further legitimate departure from the movement. It provides a contrasting set of ideas and beliefs from which to discredit the old plausibility structure while reinforcing the individual's new social location. In this way, the defection process should be understood as a legitimating sequence in which each phase or aspect of detachment needs to be justified or rationalized. This is made much easier if the individual can find a social support structure which helps to encourage disaffiliation.

I am not suggesting that transformations are always immediate and total after one leaves the group. As individuals depart to enter a different movement or re-enter the dominant culture, adoption of a new perspective and the development of new social relationships may be quite gradual. Ideas and beliefs obviously are changing, but the individual may still be experiencing confusion and thus lack any real identification with a new perspective or new reference group. Skonovd (1981:133-36) describes such disorientations among apostates as "floating." In my sample, approximately 40 percent appear to have been floaters, at least for a time, while 11 percent may still be described as floating. In cases where individuals have not yet firmly relocated in new plausibility structures that can provide support for redefinitions of identity and subjective reality, the legitimating sequence of transformation is incomplete. In other words, if one is not firmly rooted in an alternate plausibility structure that can supply an integrated framework for discrediting previous beliefs and practices, disorientation is likely to arise.

Social and Psychological Dislocation

Pending identification and affiliation with other social groups, re-entering society, or "the world," may seem like walking into a vacuous and meaningless social void for some defectors.

It took me a long time to get readjusted to doing things on my own, making my own decisions, not being told what to do or how to do it. You know you really get used to that, and then suddenly you're out on your own and you are not really sure where to go or what to do. . . . People can seem so cold and uncaring. Everybody is so busy rushing around, just into their own selfish trips. They don't care about anyone else but themselves. It's all so damn meaningless. So you start thinking, "Maybe I'm making a mistake, maybe I shouldn't have left," you know (Interview #43).

When the individual has no specific social location upon re-entry, feelings of aliena-tion and estrangement are common. There is no support structure to reinforce the individual's changed attitudes and to reassure him/her that the decision to leave was a correct one. The defector's decision to leave, therefore, may become tenuous and uncertain in the face of impersonal and alienating forces in the larger social world. This kind of vacillation can provoke attitudes of resignation or cynicism towards life ("It's all so damn meaningless."). Consequently, the role of a new support structure, to help reduce vacillating tendencies and affirm a new perspective, is critical.

Moreover, re-entry does not mean simply returning to one's previous lifestyle and identity before joining a world-transforming movement. Because of the substantial changes one might expect to experience from involvement in this kind of movement, returning to a pre-conversion plausibility structure may prove to be an impossible task. One defector's account reveals the difficulty of such an attempt.

When I finally left the church, I went back to North Carolina and got a job as a hotel clerk. I rented an apartment and just tried to resume my life. But that was a mistake. Everything was different. You know, I had been away for four years. All the people I'd known in high school were married and some of them had kids. I don't know, I just couldn't relate to all that. They were all the same people and everything, but I guess I was different. I had been through so much, and here were these people sitting around drinking and talking about football and hunting and buying new cars and all this. Who the hell cares about football or going hunting? What does that have to do with anything? I don't know, I felt like I was from another world. . . . I just didn't have anything in common with them anymore (Interview #20).

Some persons who attempt to recapture or rebuild old friendships and social ties may be sorely disappointed. Like the principal character in Thomas Hardy's novel, *Return of the Native*, one finds that he or she "can't go home." Travisano (1981:239), in a study of identity changes among converts to Messianic Judaism, states the same problem in a different way: "The black sheep who return to the fold are somehow different from those who never left." The prodigal son or daughter returns as a different person, bringing an entirely different set of experiences and values into the situation. Changes cannot be erased or ignored and the individual soon discovers that he or she can no longer identify with the people or the community they left years before. Situa-tions such as this create marked social and psychological dislocation for some defec-tors making the process of transition particularly difficult.

Reintegration is made possible by mediating plausibility structures that offer ave-nues of resocialization and aid adaptation of individuals to mainstream culture. These may include family or kinship networks, occupational groups, colleges or universities, former friends, or alternate religious groups. However, certain social groups and per-spectives are better "equipped" to accommodate such individuals. They simply have better resources and provisions to assimilate prior experiences of defectors, to provide pertinent information and knowledge, and to identify new directions, thereby facilitating readjustment. Here I refer to religious groups that appear to have better success in assimilating cognitively "old" and "new" perspectives into a comprehensive whole.

It may come as no surprise that a majority of defectors in this study joined other religious groups after leaving a world-transforming movement. "Religiously musical" persons (to borrow a Weberian metaphor) are likely to be more empathetic about the experiences and events of the defector's life. After all, one remains in the same "universe of discourse," if one continues to have a religious orientation to life. Indeed, the conservative religious groups to which most defectors were drawn share some common characteristics with world-transforming movements. Let us now turn our attention to this particular avenue of reintegration.

Reintegration Through Conservative Religious Groups

As stated in chapter five, my data indicate that 78 percent of the defectors in the sample reported at least some commitment to another religious group or belief-system. Slightly more than half (53%) of the sample were active in conservative fundamentalist/ evangelical or charismatic (neo-Pentecostal) religious groups.[1] All indications point to the fact that the latter were persons with a strong religious orientation. During the interviews, they were vocal and unapologetic about their new identity and beliefs, while those not identifying as fundamentalists/evangelicals or charismatics (the remaining 25%) were more likely to see religion as one component—though not an unimportant one—of their new social location and perspective.

Those *not* identifying with conservative religious groups reportedly did not want to repeat the "mistake" of becoming involved in an organization that would make unreasonably high demands on their personal time and energy. Many of these persons were also those rediscovering latent interests such as school or family. Religion was seen as important, but they did not want formal involvements to interfere with other pursuits. While maintaining religious convictions, they were content to remain unaffiliated with any specific religious organization or church. The following two quotes illustrate the attitudes found among this group of defectors:

> I never thought I would really ever come to this point, but . . . I'm kind of relaxed about the whole thing now. I used to be just really gung-ho, you know. Always reading things and really talking to people, going to church, and so forth. All these sort of things. But now I'm just kind of taking it easy. I'm more content with my life than I ever have been before, although I don't intend to go to church (Interview #37).

> I don't think I will ever really be involved with a church again. My religious beliefs—well, I still consider myself a religious person. . . . I guess I just have a vague belief in God. It is a strong belief, but I don't have all the details worked out, and I don't think I ever will (Interview #15).

Persons returning to school or attempting to recover family ties may want to take an extended "holiday" from intense religious involvement and affiliation. Their attitudes may be compared to those experiencing "burn-out" among religious professionals (Jud, Burch, and Mills, 1970). Nonetheless, the majority of defectors who report a continued religious orientation, turn to groups which make similarly high demands upon their lives. One must ask why?

Conservative fundamentalist/evangelical or charismatic religious groups offer avenues of resocialization and reintegration that are especially appropriate and unique to former members of world-transforming movements. They represent ideal locations on the cognitive map. The cultural and ideological coordinates of conservative religious groups in American society permit re-entry of defectors without disallowing intense religiosity. In effect, they offer manageable "terms" of reintegration allowing the individual to maintain a high level of religious commitment and belief while also permitting, and even encouraging, secular social participation and involvement. Communal organization is replaced by more democratic forms of church polity and individuals are typically encouraged to pursue secular occupations and careers. Promotion of the "work ethic" and other dominant social values is not uncommon among such groups (Dearman, 1974; Hargrove, 1979:231; Johnson, 1961; Jorstad, 1981). Indeed, conservative religious groups may even boast of their ability to successfully socialize members in values that subsequently produce good employees (Fowler, 1982:26-34).[2]

By the same token, fundamentalist religious groups also maintain a degree of social distinctiveness within the larger culture by virtue of their particular religious beliefs and practices. This distinctiveness may sometimes involve a moral posture that stands against the values or practices of the dominant culture (e.g., prohibitions against divorce, premarital sex, profanity, gambling, alcohol, etc.). Therefore, the ideologies of these conservative religious organizations do, in fact, share similarities with world-transforming movements regarding the rejection of certain elements of mainstream culture. Essentially, fundamentalism/evangelical or charismatic groups are socially positioned in-between the polarities of total rejection and total acceptance of the social order ("Be ye in the world, but not of it."). Re-entering defectors may affiliate with conservative religious groups without totally embracing the values and lifestyle of secular culture.

The avenue of social reintegration offered by these groups may be seen as leading more in the direction of what Weber (1958) calls a "this-worldly asceticism"—an acting out of a rationalistic and activist religious faith *within* the social order. This type of religious expression sees mundane activities such as one's work or career as a "calling" to carry out God's will in the course of daily interaction and involvement in social life. Believers are admonished to be the "salt of the earth," thus gradually transforming society by their influence and example (Minnery and Kantzer, 1982:10-11). Unlike the ideology of world-transforming movements this perspective holds that social change is slow or gradual and is accomplished within existing social, political, and economic institutions.[3]

World-transforming movements tend to emphasize the extreme differences between the corrupted social order and the special moral status of the group. But the conservative evangelical groups redefine the role of the believer as one who must seek to be a positive moral and spiritual influence within the institutional framework of society. In doing so, they help provide religious legitimation for the social structure, thereby perpetuating acceptance or tolerance of prevailing institutions and aiding the process of reintegration.

This explanation essentially holds that a transition vis-à-vis conservative religious groups is easier to accomplish because it is, so to speak, a "shorter step" toward reintegration. As such, reintegration is not a complete reversal of one's former identity, lifestyle, and worldview. Travisano (1981:239) argues that a transformation "back and forth between antithetic total universes of discourse is a rare possibility." But when social reintegration is legitimated by entry through a highly religious plausibility structure, ideological mobility is facilitated. Joining a fundamentalist/evangelical or charismatic religious group serves to make social relocation less difficult, requiring fewer or less radical changes.

One way in which this is demonstrated is by analyzing who is most likely to use this mode of reintegration. Table 7.1 shows that that largest percentage of defectors joining conservative fundamentalist groups were those leaving the Children of God (31%, N = 14), while the smallest percent were former Hare Krishna devotees (9%, N = 4). Unification Church defectors constituted the remaining 13 percent (N = 16) of those who fell into this category. This finding provides additional support for the "shorter step" explanation. Of the three movements, the Children of God share the most similarities with conservative fundamentalist/evangelical and charismatic groups (Richardson and Davis, 1981; Richardson and Reidy, 1980; Richardson, et al., 1979). Its roots are firmly implanted in the fundamentalist tradition. The Children of God began as a radical faction of the Jesus Movement, led by a former Christian and Missionary Alliance pastor (Richardson and Davis, 1983; Richardson et al., 1979; Wallis, 1979). There is also evidence that fundamentalist and neo-Pentecostal churches have been successful in absorbing the greatest remnants of the Jesus movement (Richardson and Reidy, 1980). Thus, one might expect to find this avenue of reintegration more readily used by ex-members of the Children of God. For these defectors, fundamentalist groups offer a viable path to sustaining religious integrity while one's relocation is being sought. Some degree of continuity can be maintained among these individuals because they can still claim to be "Bible-believing Christians" before and after disaffiliating from the movement. On the other hand, the Hare Krishna would appear to be least like fundamentalist Christian groups, originating in India and deriving most of its religious teachings and practices from Hinduism. The slightly higher number of Unification Church defectors may be attributed to the fact that the movement borrows from both Eastern and Western religious traditions.

Table 7.1	DEFECTORS JOINING FUNDAMENTALIST ORGANIZATIONS BY FORMER AFFILIATION	
	% of All Defectors	(N)
Children of God	31	(14)
Unification Church	13	(6)
Hare Krishna	9	(4)
Total =	54	(24)

In making the adjustment to a new life outside of the movement, the final stage of the legitimation sequence is critical to complete the transformation of identity and subjective reality. The adoption of an alternate plausibility structure enables the individual to "put the past behind him/her." It validates disengagement and re-entry and firmly places the individual in his or her new social location. The following account illustrates the role of the alternate plausibility structure in completing transition. This particular case involves a former member of the Children of God who eventually adopted an evangelical belief system and support structure. The defector, Mike, suggests that his former beliefs were not completely discredited until association and identification with this new group was made.

. . . I went back to Illinois and got a job. I got a job as an assistant manager at Walgreens and we started having Bible studies in our home, I got involved in a coffeehouse. . . . I taught there a couple of times, became kind of a known figure there. I just really saw that maybe this is why God wanted me out, because we used to have studies and up to forty people were in our house. All those people that we were dealing with, they were teenagers, they were just in high school at the time. . . . But that's when—when I came back from over in Europe, that's when I was really broken and I really started contemplating that maybe God works outside the Children of God. . . .

When I was in Illinois I came across a group of Christians that were from all over the Southwest, Midwest, and Northwest, and they were having this big conference. They were renting out the University of Tennessee and they were kind of gathering for a week's teaching, and then they were going back to different locations for the summer (summer training institutes and workshops). They all had their different churches and different jobs. But the principles—a gal came to one of our studies who was going to that and she shared with me and Elaine the principles that these different fellowships were emphasizing. And for the first time, I saw, outside of the Children of God, that there were other groups who really valued community, you know. Who really valued discipleship, who really valued the teachings of Christ and acknowledged them and sought to live by them. And I was very excited. . . . So I quit my job in a couple of months and we went down to this conference, and that summer we spent with this group from Kansas. . . . I heard people talking about, like, the Children of God, and stuff like that and challenging certain views from the Scripture that they had held. And I was kind of listening from the sidelines, you know, and just considering the things they were saying, and thinking, "That really makes sense."

So my exposure to this group of Christians challenged points that had been taught to me as gospel truth, and I really saw that their stance from the Scripture on these things was really much more solid than my blind obedience to them, to the things they were challenging. So that was very instrumental in my life, the summer I spent with these people (Interview #9).

The processes of transition and reintegration moved toward completion as Mike began to identify with and adopt the new religious plausibility structure. After leaving the Children of God, he expressed uncertainty about his decision and explicitly indicated a need to find a theological rationale for the new direction his life was taking (". . . I really started contemplating that maybe God works outside the Children of God.") At this point, he implied that he was still looking for some support of his actions. A significant sign of affirmation emerged with the discovery of another group of highly committed evangelical Christians. As identification with this group congealed, the remaining vestiges of the old reality were discredited and a new perspective and lifestyle were born.

Though the data show that defectors from the Children of God were most likely to attach themselves to conservative religious groups, there also appears to be some element of attraction for other defectors as well. Ten defectors from the other two movements (six ex-Unification Church members and four ex-Hare Krishnas) also chose this avenue of reintegration. Figuratively speaking, we may view these faiths as "dialects" of the same (religious) language. The existence of a spiritual or religious focus in the process of transformation of this type can easily be translated and understood, in terms of traditional biblical imagery, as a "spiritual journey" toward ultimate truth or salvation. One may believe he or she is on the road to salvation and that God will safely lead the individual to his/her proper destination. An example of this perspective can be seen in the following account by a former devotee of the Hare Krishna movement:

I am a born-again Christian now so I've realized the vast difference between

Christ, who he really is, and Christ, who I thought he was back then, and just the whole difference in a relationship with God and whatever I had back then. I don't know, the difference is like night and day. Really. . . .

INTERVIEWER: When did you have your Christian experience? How long after you left the Hare Krishnas?

RESPONDENT: It was a few years, because this happened about two years ago that I became a Christian. . . . In the interim I was just going back to SRF, you know, Self-Realization Fellowship, . . . and I was just about to get into parapsychology, you know, before I became a Christian, so God really spared me from that. . . . I was really spiritually searching and I think God just saw that and he reached down and touched me.

. . . There's really no comparison now. The freedom and the love compared to the—not the servitude, but the slavery, kind of back then, and when it's forced, you know: "You gotta love him." And in a way it was very, very hard to love Krishna because he was so bizarre, you know, you couldn't relate to God so easily. . . . It was just weird relating to God back then, I didn't really feel like I knew him personally like I do now (Interview #44).

Among accounts such as this, there is unquestionably a sense in which the individual's new beliefs help to "seal" one's past, to close the books on one's former career and to enable one to view it as only a temporary episode in the individual's life. Thus, it is in the context of the new plausibility structure that the "vast difference" between Krishna and Christ is realized. The former perspective is thoroughly repudiated and disarmed of its interpretive validity by the individual's new faith. Defection is complete. The old life is history. The individual begins a new life, as the phrase "born-again" so vividly suggests. But to experience rebirth, one must "die" to one's old life. Consider the following biblical passage often recited by fundamentalists and evangelicals in this context:

Therefore if any man be in Christ, he is a new creature, old things are passed away; behold, all things are become new (II Corinthians 5:17, KJV).

The rebirth arises out of rejecting or "dying" to one's previous identity, lifestyle, and worldview, and most defectors who joined these religious groups were quick to point out the renunciation of their former affiliation and beliefs.

Other Avenues of Reintegration

Though religion played a major role in aiding reintegration, there were other support structures identified by defectors as well. In some cases, they were altogether exclusive of religion, while among others they were sought in conjunction with another religious perspective.

A few defectors (13%) endeavored to invest themselves in new careers or occupational pursuits. Of course, occupational groups frequently provide their own distinctive types of role identities, lifestyles, and support structures (Simpson and Simpson, 1981; Van Maanen and Schein, 1979). Submerging oneself in a new job may have the effect of helping an individual forget about the past, as well as providing a chance for a new start. A new identity may be established around the occupational role. The individual who assumes such a role is immediately placed in a structured network of relations which can open up opportunities to gain new friends. Essentially, the defector has access to a whole new social world through the work setting. As one defector said,

> I don't know about anybody else, but for me, a lot of it (getting readjusted) was just finding a good job, getting back into circulation and meeting people. No one at work knew I had been a Moonie, so it's like that didn't exist (Interview #19).

The work setting may also be simply a place to "bury" oneself while a gradual process of readjustment is being negotiated. Individuals may feel like getting "lost" in a job for a period of time in order to work out problems of transition and identity change. In this kind of situation, the work place can become a sanctuary or asylum for persons who want to dissociate themselves from religion entirely. The following comments by one defector are an example of this attitude.

> . . . [T]hat was the best thing that could have happened to me (finding a job). I didn't have to talk to anybody about anything except what was related to my job. I kept myself busy and I didn't really have the time to dwell on my problems. The only thing I had to do was to go to work in the morning, earn my paycheck, and then come home at night (Interview #43).

For persons who want to shed their former identities and avoid questions about the past, the work setting may allow defectors to become absorbed in the work role. The comments from the account above indicate that submergence in a job may allow one to escape unwanted inquiries and maintain a strictly occupational identity to one's peers, at least for an initial period of time. The "busy-ness" of job-related duties and responsibilities disallows penetration of the defector's biography.

Reintegration may also be sought through universities or colleges. Seven ex-members (16%) reported returning to school in order to complete a college degree or find a career. Such environments may provide very effective mediating plausibility structures for persons wanting to chart a new course for his or her life. Indeed, universities are very appropriate social settings for these kinds of personal changes. They are accepted as legitimate repositories of knowledge and learning, and thus constitute unique social locations for preparatory socialization or training. Ex-members may be drawn to these institutions in an effort to locate new interests and goals and acquire new ideas and skills for one's future, as well as gain a different perspective on past experiences. According to one defector,

> I came back here in '76 and started school in the fall. . . . I had a double major in political science and economics. I figured that if I put in just half as much time (studying) as I did selling flowers, I would be finished in no time. I suppose that was one good thing that came out of all that. You learn how hard you can push yourself, if you have to (Interview #16).

It may also be argued that colleges and universities are recognized places for being legitimately unsure of a direction. Defectors who are undecided about career choices or what skills are needed to prepare for the future may choose to return to school to explore opportunities. This avenue of reintegration permits the defector to be in a "holding pattern" while decisions are made. The remarks made by one defector are relevant to this point.

> I went back to school for a year and a half after I left. I'm working right now . . . [but] I will be going back to school in January. . . . I'm not sure what kind of degree I'll get but I'm going to try and work with an interdisciplinary thing involving

speech communication. . . . I have to talk with more counselors about it. Anyway, it's not worked out yet (Interview #15).

One additional reason for the selection of this mode of relocation might be hypothesized. The university, like conservative fundamentalist groups, occupies a distinctive niche in society. Unlike fundamentalist groups, however, it is an environment conducive to experimentation and change. There is a greater tolerance for unpopular or unconventional ideas. The university is generally committed, in principle, to the free exchange of ideas and the protection of the rights of minority views. Therefore, one might assume that there would be less stigma attached to an individual who has been involved in a controversial religious movement. Students may even convert these biographical experiences into productive assets, writing term papers, leading or enlivening group discussions or searching out related fields of study which utilize insights and wisdom gained (e.g., counseling, psychology, sociology, communications). It is worth noting in relation to Skonovd's (1981:175) finding that "many" of the defectors he interviewed also "were still pursuing undergraduate, graduate, or professional degrees."

Another avenue of reintegration taken by defectors is through family or kinship groups. Eight defectors (18%) fell into this category. Not all defectors have close ties with their families before joining, nor seek reconciliation after leaving. For others, their involvement in the movement has had the effect of deteriorating what closeness they once might have had with their families (see Beckford, 1982; Levine, 1984). But some defectors do seek to reestablish family bonds, and identify this tie as an important source of support in the process of transition and readjustment. The following comments by one ex-member are indicative of this.

My folks were very supportive through the whole thing. I don't mean they were glad I was a devotee. But they didn't flip out when I joined the movement and I think they honestly tried to understand why I was doing it, you know. Some of the parents reacted really badly and tried to kidnap their kids—as if that was going to help their relationship any. I think I would have really resented that. . . . The big thing was that they just kept loving me and I always knew I had that if I ever decided to leave (Interview #39).

In some cases, parents or families may offer more than simply emotional or moral support. Family support may also include financial aid or assistance in securing employment. Since defectors have little or no money when they leave, such aid can be a significant source of encouragement and help. The following remarks by two defectors point to this type of family support.

It's pretty hard when you first leave. You know, you don't have any money or anything. I know my parents helped us some at first (Interview #14).

My dad, he helped get me a job with this friend of his, doing construction work. It didn't pay all that well, but for me it seemed like a lot of money at the time. . . . It helped me to get on my feet (Interview #32).

As was discussed in chapter five, family ties can be a vital link in the transformational process. But more than just a factor in the decision-making phase, families can provide support structures or networks when social relocation is sought. They offer alternative social bases from which to find encouragement to start over and build a new life. Where parent-child disagreements over affiliation have not dissolved the relationship and lines of communication have remained open, the family can help ease the strain of adjustment. To be sure, defectors rarely return home to live with their parents or families, usually maintaining a separate residence and a self-determined resolve to manage their own affairs. They insist on making their own decisions and want to be regarded as independent and capable adults. Familial support should not be confused with parental dominance or control. Voluntary defectors are individuals who already have demonstrated considerable initiative and independence by the act of disaffiliation. They merely seek respect and approbation to bolster their reintegrative efforts. In this role, however, there is no doubt that families can supply deep emotional support and affirmation which surpasses most other types of groups.

In summary then, defection is not simply a process of detachment but also one of social and psychological relocation. I have identified briefly how defectors cultivate or pioneer different avenues of reintegration. In the next chapter I want to turn to an examination of post-involvement attitudes towards one's former group. How do these individuals feel about having been involved in a cultic movement? Do they feel exploited? Do they think they were brainwashed? How are these emotions and attitudes assimilated?

CHAPTER EIGHT

LOOKING BACK: POST-INVOLVEMENT EVALUATIONS
AND ATTITUDES

Major changes or life-transitions can be difficult for many people in contemporary society. Entering adolescence, dissolving an intimate relationship, going off to college, entering the Armed Services, getting married, finding a career, having children, overcoming a mid-life crisis, changing jobs, moving to a different part of the country, struggling through a divorce or retirement are just a few examples. These kinds of transitions are normal parts of the life-cycle and yet they can be terribly stressful and impose formidable periods of readjustment for countless persons. Defectors from world-transforming movements are also experiencing major life-transitions. Like so many others, they are undergoing some fundamental changes in their private lives.

For many observers, however, involvement in such groups or movements is seen as qualitatively different. While research strongly suggests that attrition rates are quite high for most new religions, objections are continually being raised about the *effects* of involvement. These objections take several different forms. For example, participation in a new religious movement is often seen as a needless detour resulting in a waste of human resources and time, taking "individuals out of conventional social networks and career paths and leading to the inculcation of individual qualities inconsistent with a competitive, economic achievement orientation" (Shupe and Bromley, 1980:37). In other words, participation involves a *deviant* lifestyle, identity, and worldview wherein youth may squander important educational and occupational opportunities. Involvement may also be seen as a waste of emotional and psychological energies. Like other life-transitions, it may be emotionally painful or disturbing for the participant, as well as to close friends and relatives. Some observers have even gone so far as to claim discovery of peculiar side-effects. Margaret Singer, a clinical psychologist states it this way (1979:75):

> Leaving any restricted community can pose problems—leaving the Army for civilian life is hard, too, of course. In addition, it is often argued that people who join cults are troubled to begin with, and that the problems we see in postcult treatment are only those postponed by conversion and adherence. . . . But some residues that some of these cults leave in many ex-members seem special: slipping into dissociated states, severe incapacity to make decisions, and related extreme suggestibility derive, I believe, from the effects of specific behavior conditioning practices on some especially susceptible persons.

Whether or not transitions of this type are any more destructive or psychologically difficult than some others—particularly the Army (see Goffman, 1961)—is at least debatable.[1] Mental health professionals, such as the one cited above, have come under extensive criticism for this kind of "medicalization of deviance" approach to new religions (Hargrove, 1980; Robbins, 1979, 1981; Robbins and Anthony, 1980a, 1980b). Highly subjective characterizations of mental aberrations among ex-members may often derive from very questionable assumptions about "mind control" and "brainwashing."

But several important questions do arise about the impact of membership upon individuals after they leave world-transforming movements. For example: What do these persons feel and think about their previous involvement in such groups? What kinds of attitudes do they hold upon reflection? Are they angry? Confused? Do they really feel they were brainwashed? How are these experiences interpreted? And are they seen in a positive or negative manner?

Many of these questions have been explored in previous research (Beckford, 1978; Clark, 1979; Clark, et al., 1981; Conway and Seigelman, 1978; Galanter, 1983; Skonovd, 1981; Singer, 1979; Solomon, 1981), but the findings often have not been clear. The problem is due, in part, to the failure of most studies to distinguish between the responses of deprogrammed persons and voluntary defectors (for an exception, see Galanter, 1983b). By voluntary defectors, I want to reiterate that I am referring to those persons who have left without the aid of deprogramming of "exit therapy" (Solomon, 1981). For example, studies by Conway and Seigelman (1978), Clark (1979), and Singer (1979) rely predominantly on accounts by deprogrammed individuals. In another study, Skonovd (1981) combines the accounts of deprogrammed individuals and voluntary defectors and therefore fails to recognize a very important distinction. This methodological oversight presents a serious problem. Solomon (1981) has shown that persons who are successfully deprogrammed tend to adopt, as reference groups, anticult organizations which promote brainwashing theories of conversion. As a result, these accounts are often infused with conspiratorial assumptions about "mind control" and techniques of psychological manipulation generating what Shupe and Bromley (1980) have called "atrocity tales." However, one must seriously question the validity of such explanations, particularly the language or conceptual framework of these accounts, when the respondents have undergone some type of deprogramming or comparable therapeutic treatment. At least it remains an empirical question as to whether such explanations characterize accounts by defectors who have left of their own volition, without such assistance.

It is also indicated by Solomon's study that further investigation of the subject is needed due to the small number of persons in her sample (7%) who did not undergo any deprogramming or therapy (the latter employed often after legal conservatorships had been obtained). Indeed, Solomon (1981:291) admits to a possible bias in this regard.

The small number of voluntary subjects in the sample might be attributed to the common belief that it is impossible to leave the (Unification) Church without assistance. However, there is such a ready supply of trained and untrained people anxious to be of assistance to members upon exit, services rendered are not so much sought out as given freely—though usually for a fee. In addition, the lack of purely voluntary subjects may be due to sampling bias because it is extremely difficult to successfully track down members who left voluntarily and who have never been in contact with the ex-member network.

The sample of voluntary defectors used in this study has an obvious advantage. None of the respondents here have experienced any of the exit treatments found in prior studies. Though some may have come into contact with anticult literature after their departure, there are no reported experiences with deprogramming or exit therapy that served to aid defection.

To assess post-involvement attitudes and reactions, the following question was asked of voluntary defectors:

When you think about having been a member, how do you feel? Indifferent?___
Angry?___ Duped/Brainwashed?___ Wiser for the experience?___ How do you
feel?

The interview question was designed to elicit a specific response, but also to permit the individual to modify or elaborate upon the response in order to insure a better communication of his or her attitudes and thoughts.

A summary of the findings are shown in Table 8.1. One may indeed find these results surprising, given the claims of previous studies. The data show that a full two-thirds (67%) of the defectors interviewed could look back with some degree of social and emotional distance and say they felt "wiser for the experience." Though this mode of response requires some careful explanation of content, a much different pattern of post-involvement attitudes is evident among voluntary defectors. Attitudes and reactions emerge which are typically more tolerant and less critical of one's previous group than other research would indicate.

Table 8.1	POST-INVOLVEMENT RESPONSES OF VOLUNTARY DEFECTORS	
Response	%	*N*
Angry	7	(3)
Duped/Brainwashed	9	(4)
Wiser for the experience	67	(30)
Indifferent	0	(0)
Other	18	(8)
Total	101	(45)

Before exploring the specific responses of subjects, some explanation of this pattern seems in order. The voluntary defection process itself should help to explain the greater levels of tolerance and understanding exhibited by these individuals. Unlike deprogrammed persons who encounter relentless, mediated reconstructions of cult involvement by deprogrammers in a brief period of hours or days, voluntary defectors often experience a disengagement sequence that will last for months. Consequently, the time frame allows for a *gradual* process in which determination of a new direction in one's life may be weighed carefully and judiciously. The process is not at all unlike that identified by family researchers regarding divorce. Research shows that individuals preparing to separate from a spouse often begin forming independent careers, objectives, and lifestyles far in advance of the final confrontation or event (Chiriboga and Thurner, 1980; Federico, 1979; Goode, 1956; Thompson and Spanier, 1983; Weiss, 1975). For example, Weiss (1975:17) reports that women caught in failing marriages frequently wait until they obtain paid employment before departing. One woman interviewed by Weiss waited until she completed the college work required for a nursing degree before leaving her husband. In a similar vein, studies of marital dissolution are replete with accounts of disaffected spouses who postpone divorce until the children are grown. These studies suggest that careful deliberations of costs and rewards are likely to elicit more pensive, clearheaded responses. The same is true of the defection process, as I believe the data will show.

In contrast, Spanier and Casto (1979:218) find that the degree to which marital separation is sudden and unexpected is related to negative emotional reactions. Like the abandoned spouse, the deprogrammed individual may feel betrayed by the group if successfully persuaded that he or she has been duped or manipulated. It is reasonable to assume, therefore, that in the absence of a lengthier, undisturbed process of re-examination and self-determined detachment, initially formed perceptions of betrayal (mediated, of course, by deprogrammers) contribute to more negative reactions among deprogrammed persons. This would account for the harsher tone of reports by these individuals. For example, Singer (1979) reports a notable inability among deprogrammed youth to discuss positive aspects of their experience in the group. Galanter (1983b:986) finds that "the responses of deprogrammed former members also reflected greater alienation from the Unification Church, compared with ex-members who were not deprogrammed." The voluntary defector, in contrast, has had more solitary time to weigh the decision, to consider alternatives, and to build an entirely different rationale for leaving.

This was, in fact, evident in the content of the responses to the questionnaire item. Defectors were frequently sympathetic and philosophical about their involvements. They often retained some ambivalent admiration for the movement or recounted highly valued experiences or relationships. Even in detailing numerous legitimate reasons for leaving, one sensed in their answers a felt loss of closeness, unity, and cooperation in achieving shared goals or ideals. As some stated, this did not necessarily mean they would repeat the experience, given the opportunity to choose again. What it did mean was that they often believed it was a "learning" or "growing experience." The following responses were typical of this type of attitude.

I think I'm wiser for the experience. I don't feel duped, . . . I think it was a real period of growth, and I feel much richer for the experience. I think some of their ideals were very valid and I think they were a very giving, a very loving group. In a way, I kind of regret that I couldn't have given as much as they wanted (Interview #13).

I really feel wiser for the experience, because you know, there were really a lot of nice people and you really learned a lot of lessons. You learned a lot of things; how not to treat people, you learned how to be more understanding. You know, once you are in that situation, you can really see how it is. Although, at times, you feel kind of stupid for having done it, still, at the same time, you learned a whole lot, and there were really a lot of good people we met . . . that I wish we could meet them again. I wish they had left (too) (Interview #14).

I'm not angry, you know, because it was of my own volition that I was there and I could have just walked out anytime. You know, I know that. But I guess I'm grateful that God allowed me to have that experience because after that I was totally free of the philosophy. . . . [I]t was a hard experience and maybe I was crazy for doing it, but I was just grateful that I had gotten it out of my system and I could go on to other things (Interview #44).

I really feel I'm wiser for it. I wouldn't trade it, . . . it was just such an experience, and I've talked to other ex-COG's and they feel the same way (Interview #34).

I feel pretty good about it (laughing). . . . Sure there was a lot of stuff that wasn't correct and we did get to the bottom of it, I think. But we just can't negate or nullify all the hundreds of people we lived with and really loved dearly and just— we feel so close to them. We got to know another country, another culture; we lived in Germany for four years, you know. We feel like it is our second home. We feel that even in our relationship with the Lord, it really made us stronger and really helped us to maybe be a little more streetwise to what's going on. I don't know, I just—I know a lot of people are bitter, but I guess I don't feel bitter, against anybody in particular. . . . I have a hard time holding strong ill feelings against anyone . . . and there was so much good. . . . That's not to condone what they are practicing, but we don't look back on it and say, "Oh, we just shot four years, wasted, you know" (Interviews #7, 8).

As seen by these remarks, defectors often indicated a sustained affection or appreciation for certain aspects of group involvement, particularly with regard to the development and maintenance of close, interpersonal relationships within the movement. Defectors frequently pointed to elements that approximated primary group interaction. For example, when asked if the group was like or unlike a "family" to them, most respondents were able to draw meaningful comparisons between the group and their biological families.

In chapter four, it was found that defectors rarely attributed their disillusionment to a lack of affectivity among group members. The data suggest that these movements have tended to serve as primary or quasi-primary groups for their adherents. Despite unorthodox beliefs and practices, communal groups can provide unique settings for developing emotionally satisfying relationships within a society characterized by impersonal bureaucratic structures (Hillery, 1981). However, when individuals leave these groups, they often find it extremely difficult to recreate similar intimate relationships in the larger society. Perhaps it is not surprising, then, to find that some defectors will adamantly disagree with their former groups on ideological or theological grounds, seeing them as misguided or spiritually adrift, while retaining a positive recollection of deep, interpersonal relationships.

For a few, this same mode of response ("wiser for the experience") was a way of saying that they had been able to salvage some positive things out of something essentially seen as negative. They perceived their choice, in retrospect, as a mistake, yet they also could see some redeeming value in their involvement with the movement. The following comments compare the defector's own experience to that of the biblical character, Job.

Well, because now I'm a Christian, I believe God allows us, in his infinite wisdom and his mercy, to experience certain things in our lives. I believe he allowed that to happen to me because just as he allowed Satan to touch Job, he allowed that to happen to me. Because of the involvement I had with them, I have a very deep burden for people not only in the Krishna movement but in cults, in general. . . . I believe he allowed it to happen—I won't say it was a "good" experience, but God turned a bad experience around and made it into a good experience. I can share with people in cults. I can identify with them a little, you know; know what they are going through (Interview #45).

These comments aptly suggest that one may also feel "wiser for the experience" without particularly cherishing one's past commitment. However, even allowing for the variation of responses within the category of "wiser for the experience," what is readily demonstrated in these findings is the almost complete absence of "brainwashing" accusations. Attitudes are markedly less dogmatic and less odious than previous research has suggested. Accounts by voluntary defectors are generally characterized by greater tolerance and flexibility in arriving at an understanding of one's previous involvement. Unlike their deprogrammed counterparts, these former members rarely claim that their participation in the groups is a product of psychological manipulation. Only 9 percent of those interviewed chose to describe their participation and commitment in this way. Conversely, 91 percent of the sample felt their participation was entirely voluntary and specifically avoided the language and rhetoric of brainwashing. To my knowledge, all of the respondents were aware of the controversy, and many were quite critical of the term "brainwashing" altogether.

For those who reconceptualized their involvement in the brainwashing motif, explanations typically revolved around allegedly sophisticated techniques of mind control and psychophysiological manipulation. The following comments by one defector shared common conceptual elements found in accounts by deprogrammed persons (Conway and Seigelman, 1978; Patrick, 1976) and served to illustrate the influence of acknowledged anticult contact.

I was never allowed to leave Tarryton after I arrived for about a year; nine months of which I was subjected to brainwashing techniques. . . . Everything that happens is exactly parallel to what a POW experiences, and for a certain amount of time I feel that I did not have my free will. . . . The free will is destroyed (Interview #22).

The striking contrast between the reconceptualization of the individual's experience described above and the majority of accounts by defectors attest to the former's adoption of a very different interpretive framework from which to view her past involvement. Essentially, the individual's response moves beyond description, it is a theoretical "explanation" of involuntary participation or coercive persuasion (Lifton, 1961:419-37; Schein, et al., 1961). Accounts which seek to compare socialization procedures of new religions with "thought reform" techniques practiced in Chinese POW camps is quite common among anticult organizations (Shupe and Bromley, 1980:71). Both the sharpness of the contrast in accounts, and the relative scarcity of such claims in the sample, suggest adoption of a reference group ideology similar to that in Solomon's (1981) study. The example cited here, however, differs in the sequence of contact and indicates the possibility of voluntary defectors accepting the idea of involuntary participation or brainwashing.

Approximately 7 percent of those interviewed said they were "angry" about having made extensive sacrifices for the movement, and yet, had nothing to show for it. These individuals did not go so far as to claim to be brainwashed, but tended to feel that valuable time and energy was wasted. One defector said he felt "cheated" because he had "lost" several important years in his life (Interview #21). One woman complained of "chauvinistic" attitudes and practices among the male leadership in the Unification Church. Much of her anger and frustration was fueled by attitudes of a predominantly male leadership structure that she said perpetuated her own low self-esteem (Interview #30).

Some 18 percent of those interviewed responded in different ways so as to be categorized as "other." One former member of the Hare Krishna admitted to being "embarrassed" by his involvement with the group (Interview #41). Realizations about certain unethical fundraising practices in the movement reportedly generated a desire to dissociate himself entirely from the group. One defector described his reaction as "sad" because "the [Unification] Church didn't live up to its ideals" (Interview #16). Several others said they struggled with feelings of guilt, at first, for fear of having made the wrong decision; later they came to realize the group itself was "wrong" or misdirected. Still others described their feelings as "mixed" and were admittedly confused and ambivalent about their past commitments. One defector described his ambivalence toward the movement even after four and a half years of separation and reflection.

> You know, it's funny. I still have mixed feelings about the whole thing. It's just not that simple to say, well, it was all great, or it was all a bunch of shit. I'm sorry about what I put my parents through. I know they went through hell, especially my mother. But there were also a lot of positive things that I experienced during that time in my life that I'm not going to forget . . . (Interview #43).

In one sense, it might be more accurate to characterize most post-involvement attitudes as somewhat ambivalent. Even those who said they felt grateful or wiser for the experience were essentially selecting out the more commendable elements of the total experience. Beckford (1978:109) has also observed a similar ambivalence among ex-members of the Unification Church in Great Britain. He observed that defectors continued to feel "love" and "admiration" toward their former colleagues. Galanter's (1983b) research among ex-Unification Church members in the U.S. yields similar results. He found that respondents "had mixed feelings about their own membership, [and that] their responses reflected the sense that they retained a loyalty to the group and its ethos" (1983b:987). More than one ex-member in this study indicated that a sustained admiration or affection for the movement was not meant to condone immoral or unethical practices. Such expressions of ambivalence are in need of explanation.

I would like to suggest that the ambivalence of former members derives from the refusal to simplify a complex set of experiences, events, ideas, and emotional attachments. For example, strong affective ties experienced during involvement are not automatically dismissed as invalid because of subsequent ideological differences. Some elements of membership undoubtedly make lasting and favorable impressions upon defectors. Post-involvement evaluation of membership is essentially a sifting process in which favorable events or experiences are separated out from what is later perceived as wrong, immoral, or theologically adrift. As a result, one will find voluntary defectors defending certain aspects of the group while criticizing others. This kind of selectivity and separation of the more highly valued aspects of one's membership gives an indication of careful reflection on the part of the individual.

As suggested earlier, the process of defection is analogous to marital separation and divorce. Certainly, one cannot ignore the complexity of factors which contribute to marital breakdown. Neither would anyone be surprised to find among divorced persons ambivalent attitudes or mixed emotions about prior marriages. Research shows that even after marriages fail, attachments among separated persons often still persist (Spanier and Casto, 1979; Weiss, 1979). According to Weiss (1979:208-210), one of the most difficult problems among separated persons is the "management of ambivalence." For example, he states, "Most among the separated continue to feel drawn to the spouse even when a new relationship is established which appears, in many respects, satisfactory" (Weiss, 1979:203). The ambiguity of such attachments and accompanying attitudes suggest a relationship similar to that of the voluntary defector's toward his/her previous group. One's departure from the formal commitment does not erase some favorable elements nor reduce the involvement to a wholly negative experience. Even a brief marriage or religious commitment in one's biography will feature some propitious moments. In short, a comparative analysis of this type offers a much greater potential for understanding the difficulties that ex-members face, than studies focusing on POW camps.

The marital disengagement analogy highlights the psychological distress surrounding the deterioration of a previously intimate attachment. Both marriage and religious commitment require a significant degree of self-sacrifice so that when separation actually does occur, withdrawal may entail a deep sense of loss of one's self-identity. A part of the self (one's psychic investments) remains with the abandoned relationship. The estranged person feels acute emotional pain or mental anguish regardless of whether the object of that intimate association is an individual (spouse) or religious group. Consequent symptoms of loneliness, disorientation, moodiness, or what Weiss calls "separation anxiety" may be mistakenly diagnosed by clinical psychologists and psychiatrists as peculiar traits of cultic mind control when studied as unique or unparalleled phenomena. A comparative analysis of divorce and cult disinvolvement, however, reveals the short-sightedness of this myopic claim (e.g., see Galanter, 1983).

In summary, then, responses of voluntary defectors indicate that most assimilate their experiences in a constructive way and learn from them, in much the same way that individuals learn from any major social psychological transition. Whether it be from a career change, a divorce, or leaving the Armed services to re-enter civilian life, one can use these past experiences, events, and perceptions to build or guide future actions, to set different goals, and to establish new convictions.

A finding which clearly emerges from these data is a lack of support for the brainwashing argument. Regardless of how unproductive or unprofitable ex-members may view their past involvement in a new religious movement, the overwhelming majority say they were participants by their own volition. This is not to say that they did not experience the impact of a highly regulated social environment. Certainly, they did. But one need not equate this with mind control or destruction of free will. These same individuals demonstrate little difficulty in acknowledging moral inconsistencies within these movements. They are acutely aware of problems that have arisen from authoritarian leadership structures, and many of them have firsthand experiences of disillusionment as a result. But in these attitudes and assessments, one finds a position that is tempered by the extremities of both flagrant brainwashing claims and the romantic idealism of committed followers. In effect, most are faced with both positive and negative components that are not easily synthesized into one simple and harmonious explanation. The bonds of commitment that hold members to these types of movements are voluntary, even if—like the matrimonial plunge—one may not know fully what he or she is getting into.

PART FOUR
CONCLUSIONS

CHAPTER NINE

UNCONVENTIONAL RELIGION AND

MENTAL HEALTH IN THE MODERN WORLD

At the outset of this work, I claimed that "brainwashing" and coercive dissuasion of adherents to new religions were based on popular misconceptions about how commitment develops and wanes. These misconceptions derive, in part, from accounts by deprogrammed ex-members, anticult organizations, and the resulting images often perpetuated by the media (regarding the latter, see Bromley, *et. al.*, 1983; Testa, 1978). There is a tendency for the media to exploit unusual cases or to sensationalize accounts in order to sell books and newspapers, or to attract larger viewing audiences. Few people are probably aware that there is a high dropout rate among cults. Yet, the entire rationale for coercive intervention or therapeutic dissuasion rests on the assumption that members of these groups have been manipulated through brainwashing techniques that induce intense psychological and emotional dependencies upon the cult thus precluding volitional or unaided departures.[1]

The public perception of involuntary participation has grave implications for the abridgement of First Amendment rights under the Constitution (Kelly, 1977; LeMoult, 1978; Robbins, 1981, 1984, 1985b; Robbins, *et al.*, 1985; Shepherd, 1983, 1985). Members of unpopular religious groups continue to have their religious beliefs and practices impugned, often on psychiatric grounds. While such developments may only alarm a small minority of society when confined to the exclusive application of intervention techniques to stigmatized cults, the dilemma takes on new dimensions when expanded beyond these select groups. Indeed, the line distinguishing esoteric or marginal religious groups and acceptable high commitment religious groups is becoming indistinguishable (Robbins, 1985b). Trends toward secularization help recast sectarian religiosity as disreputable, making it safe only for adherents of those mainline churches with well established traditions and firmly entrenched institutional structures.

In recent years we have seen how far, under the banner of "cult brainwashing," deprogramming has been utilized to suppress unpopular or unconventional religious beliefs. With the free-wheeling and irresponsible use of the label "cult," any religious group one dislikes (e.g., Jews for Jesus, Catholic Charismatics) may be targeted for the deprogramming or psychiatric intervention.

Moreover, the effect of some deprogrammings has been to strip the individual entirely of *any* religious orientation whatsoever. My conversations with some deprogrammed ex-members revealed an outright hostility to anything religious. As one individual working with a local anticult organization in New York stated, "All religion is brainwashing." The perpetuation of this attitude, intentional or not, is to be questioned and challenged.

It is all too evident that in some instances, coercive dissuasion has had the function of creating an antireligious posture among those exposed to such treatment. Presumably, this is not the effect of what was intended. The results of this research suggest that voluntary defection does not have the far-reaching consequences of assorted intervention techniques.[2] Thus, the findings question the efficacy of deprogramming, "rehabilitation," or so-called exit therapies, if their goal is to return individuals to mainstream life with an open mind toward religious belief-systems.

There is a compelling need to recognize the adverse and harmful impact of brainwashing arguments advanced by anticult proponents, particularly those in the mental health field. Much of the literature discussing the alleged mind control technology of cults is written by psychiatrists and psychologists (Clark, 1979; Clark, et al., 1981; Galper, 1976, 1982; Miller, 1979; Shapiro, 1977; Singer, 1979; Verdier, 1977). In an increasingly secular modern world, medical and psychological models continue to encroach upon religious beliefs and experiences. One of the prominent features of modernity is that psychiatry and psychology have usurped much of the "territory" previously defined and presided over by religion (Berger, 1978; Clarke, 1979; Fromm, 1950; Rieff, 1966; Szasz, 1984; Vitz, 1977). While many people in the mental health profession do not support the overt denigration of religion nor are personally irreligious, there is unquestionably a widespread attitude in psychiatry that the medical perspective has superceded the religious perspective in explaining both the human personality and mental illness. Some outspoken critics of the medical model see some very ambitious aspirations and claims in this field, moving us closer to "the Therapeutic State." Gross (1978) contends that psychiatrists and psychologists have become an elite group of "seers" in the new "psychological society," seizing the role previously bestowed upon the clergy, philosophers, and statespersons. As we edge nearer the Therapeutic State, both private citizens and government officials become increasingly dependent on psychological experts for guidance concerning what is real or illusionary, and for a scientific standard of behavior to supplant fading traditions (see Kilbourne and Richardson, 1984). London (1964) has taken the position that psychologists are now believed to be "secular priests" who appeal to science, just as clergy make their appeals to revelation for justification of their moral prescriptions. Science has become a modern "sacred cow" wherein psychotherapists can preach codes of conduct by claiming a scientific basis for their authority. The scientific morality of modern psychology (Bergin, 1980) has succeeded to some degree in displacing the traditional clergy from the role of moral agent. Some scholars have suggested that psychotherapy and religion, particularly some new religions, are "competitors" in the therapeutic and experiential marketplace, thus explaining at least one source of social conflict (Clarke, 1979; Kilbourne and Richardson, 1984; Robbins and Anthony, 1980b, 1982).

Thomas Szasz (1970, 1974, 1984) argues that the ever-expanding mental health profession is in the process of deposing religion as the authoritative source of morality in society, superimposing medical jargon upon behavior and equating deviance with mental illness while disguising the fact that its standards and objectives are essentially moral and political. Psychiatrists and other mental health specialists are the obvious benefactors of this shifting power base, gaining the legitimate "expertise" to exercise medical opinions on no less fundamental states of reality than "sanity," "fitness," and "personality disorders." In many clinical studies, however, these states are not readily apparent, or free of ambiguity, "grey areas," and moral judgments—as the public furor over insanity testimonies by psychiatrists in the Patty Hearst and John Hinckley trials have demonstrated. According to Szasz, psychiatry dispossesses religion in the scientific technological society by "bootlegging humanistic values" under the guise of medical rhetoric.

Modern psychiatric ideology is an adaption—to a scientific age—of the traditional ideology of Christian theology. Instead of being born into sin, man is born into sickness. Instead of life being a vale of tears, it is a vale of diseases. And, as in his journey from the cradle to the grave man was formerly guided by the priest, so now he is guided by the physician. In short, whereas in the Age of Faith the ideology was Christian, the technology clerical, and the expert priestly; in the Age of Madness the ideology is medical, the technology clinical, and the expert psychiatric (Szasz, 1970:5).

The current debate over deviant religious groups is an enlightening illustration. Intense or zealous religious commitment has come to be questioned on the basis of mental health issues. What was once religious enthusiasm is now "unbalanced" extremism. The modern attitude, helped along considerably by the medical model, might be summed up in this way: "Religion is all right, if you don't take it too seriously." But is this not an attitude that reflects the demise of religious convictions and values in contemporary culture? And does this attitude not perpetuate that demise by relegating religion to a place of insignificance?

Liebman (1983) accurately observes that religious extremism, not religious moderation, traditionally has been the norm. Extremism simply refers to an orientation whereby individuals exhibit a strict adherence to a religious faith. The term "extremism" is itself value-laden, reflecting a set of criteria which give only a superfluous nod to the believability of religious meaning-systems. People who were once merely viewed as religious now qualify as extremist under the revised cultural and medical standards of modern society. But religious extremists are no real enigma. "[A] propensity to religious extremism does not require explanation," says Liebman (1983:79), "since it is entirely consistent with basic religious tenets and authentic religious orientations." Rather it is the phenomenon of religious moderation or religious liberalism that is in need of explanation. How and why do religious adherents accommodate themselves to prevailing cultural norms, or strive to make peace with the world?

Contemporary scholars point to the traits of "compromise," "civility," and "accommodation" as the major correlates of secularization (Berger, 1978; Cuddihy, 1975; Hunter, 1983). Hunter (1983:87) states that the orthodox Protestant worldview "has been culturally edited to give it the qualities of sociability and gentility. It has acquired a civility that proclaims loudly, 'No offense, I am an evangelical.' " It is in the wake of this pervasive accommodating worldview that the new religions emerged. It could be argued that religion has been so inoffensive in the last thirty years so as to become rather meaningless. Is it any wonder we saw the "Death of God" theology in the 1960s? Daniel Bell (1976:168) writes, "Where religions fail, cults appear. . . . [W]hen theology erodes and organization crumbles, when the institutional framework of religion begins to break up, the search for a direct experience which people can feel to be religious facilitates the rise of cults." Data for this study show that 75 percent of respondents were in the process of a spiritual search prior to joining a new religion. One might hypothesize that the success of these groups is due largely to the inability of mainline churches to provide opportunities for direct religious experience (Stark and Bainbridge, 1981). It is worth noting that the Unification Church had very little success in the U.S. during the early to mid-1960s. However, their membership jumped radically in the late '60s and early '70s (Lofland, 1979), a period characterized by widespread social experimentation and a search for meaning (Wuthnow, 1976).[3]

The decade of the '70s not only spawned a deep religious attraction to the cults. Many people fail to see a correlation in the parallel growth of fundamentalism or the New Religious Right. Elsewhere I have argued that the religious protest against modernity during this time encompassed *both* the rise of religious cults and the growth of fundamentalist religion (Wright, 1981). These movements must be seen as different aspects of the same phenomenon—a more widespread growth of religious dissent and unrest in the face of increasing secularization. Thus, the alarm which has been raised deriving from a narrow concentration on cults by a select group of mental health professionals ignores the complex fabric of indicators of which cults are only a small part. Taken as a whole, these movements should be seen as evident signs of cultural or structural strain. Certainly they signal extensive disillusionment with traditional religious institutions. But if the larger sociological picture is ignored, the rights and freedoms of countless religious individuals run the risk of being dealt a severe blow. As the establishment of definitions and guidelines for "normal" behavior come to be increasingly the dominion of mental health specialists, it is not too far fetched to expect in the future that any form of religious enthusiasm or commitment which exceeds acceptable standards will be subject to criticism, "treatment," and sanctions.

Right or wrong, unconventional religious groups cannot be accused of "accommodation," and it is in this context that they are most "offensive" to the modern mind. Here the battle line is drawn, and some culturally appointed representatives of the modern psyche would have these offensively dissident expressions diagnosed as evidence of "brainwashing." After all, no one in their "right" (read: modern) mind would join one of these crazy groups (to paraphrase one psychiatrist). It is a matter of indifference whether the religious belief-system is entirely novel (cultic) or historically orthodox (fundamentalist). The issue is extremism versus moderation/accommodation. It is no longer considered in the best interests of psychological well-being to be intensely religious (Richardson, 1980).

The psychological reductionism characteristic of the "brainwashing" model threatens religious freedom and belief, and is ultimately antireligious in its impact. It attacks expressions of faith wherever they are innovative or dissident and seeks to maintain a status quo religion (i.e., harmless, inoffensive, nonthreatening). This is not to defend unethical practices or abuses by new religions. Where there are obvious violations of the law (fraud or misrepresentation), steps should be taken to correct such abuses. But the bottom line is that people who want to belong to unconventional religious groups should be allowed to do so if they choose. Fabricating elaborate theories of psychological "mind control," in many instances, is simply an attempt to strip away the religious elements of unpopular beliefs in order to subject them to increased government regulation (Robbins, 1981). The strategy of such interest groups is obvious. If the beliefs and practices of unconventional religious groups can be effectively reduced to psychological dynamics, they are more likely to convince government officials to circumvent the constitutional rights of these individuals to practice their religion freely. To wit, that which is no longer "authentically" religious can not be protected by the First Amendment.

The government's growing dependence upon the mental health profession to guide political decisions and set policy should alarm those concerned with protecting religious freedoms of nontraditional groups, and by implication, *all* religious groups.[4]

One need only to turn to the political uses of psychiatry in the Soviet Union to demonstrate how arbitrarily medical symptomology and diagnoses can be devised as social weapons to suppress deviance. One of the many methods by which Soviet officials treat dissidents is to commit them to mental asylums or psychiatric colonies, justifying involuntary internment on the basis of such convenient diagnoses as "manic reformism," "psychopathic negativism," "schizophrenia," "litigation mania" (delusions of civil rights violations), and "paranoia with counterrevolutionary delusions" (Bloch and Reddaway, 1977; Conrad and Schneider, 1980; Szasz, 1984). Soviet psychiatrists see in dissidents who exhibit "reformist ideas" the formation of a latently obstinate and pathological personality. Rejecting the moral and political principles of Marxism and Communism is evaluated as a characteristic symptom of schizophrenia because political dissent reveals *de facto* a "poor adaptation to the social environment" (Bloch and Reddaway, 1977:253).

Religious dissent receives equally repressive treatment. Article 142 of the Soviet Criminal Code decrees the following acts as punishable by incarceration for one year in a labor camp: Distribution of documents calling for the nonobservance of legislation on religious cults, arousing religious superstition among the population, organization of religious meetings and ceremonies which disrupt the social order, and teaching religion to minors (Bloch and Reddaway, 1977:159). But Soviet psychiatry plays a more important role in assessing the mental health of religious individuals who participate in activities not specifically covered by Article 142. For example, conversion to a religious faith as an adult may be diagnosed as maladaptive behavior given to pathological propensities. Proscriptive treatment for such personality disorders may include compulsory internment, harassment, insulin injections and forcible use of tranquillizing drugs (Bloch and Reddaway, 1977:269). While benign religious loyalties are not typically a major concern of Soviet authorities, "expressive" or enthusiastic religion frequently incur special efforts of restriction and suffocation. Baptists, Pentecostalists, and Jews have been favorite targets of the state. Thus, the lines of demarcation distinguishing mental health from mental illness are drawn purely from *social* values and standards of behavior. Psychiatry is simply an agent of social control that functions to preserve the existing sociopolitical order. A growing body of documentation supports the claims of Soviet dissidents such as Solzhenitsyn and Sakharov that psychiatry in the USSR has become a primary tool of political and religious repression. Bloch and Reddaway suggest that psychiatry is particularly vulnerable to this type of abuse because of ill-defined boundaries.

> The nature of psychiatry is such that the potential for its improper use is greater than in any other field of medicine. Why should this be so? Several factors suggest themselves: psychiatry's boundaries are exceedingly blurred and ill-defined; little agreement exists on the criteria for defining mental illness; the mentally ill are often used as scapegoats for society's fears; and the psychiatrist commonly faces a dual loyalty, both to the patient he is treating and to the institutions to which he is responsible (Bloch and Reddaway, 1977:1).

However, the exclusive focus on Soviet psychiatry may be misleading. Szasz suggests that Western psychiatric practices are not too far removed from those of the Soviets. Psychiatric coercion also exists in the West and frequently is used to label as "mentally ill" those who do not conform to social and moral norms. According to Szasz, what many observers fail to recognize is that mental illness refers not to a medical disease but to "psychosocial" or interpersonal conflicts that routinely effect us all in day-to-day life. The mental health profession is dedicated to helping individuals adjust to their social environments. If such environments preclude or discourage sectarian religion (the prototypical "fanatic") then clinical "adjustments" may take the form of religious repression. Social and cultural environments invariably inform and shape the practices and goals of psychiatry and clinical psychology. "Wrenching analyses of psychiatric practices out of their historical, economic, and political contexts," says Szasz (1984:223), "is an exercise not only in futility but also in foolishness."

The question is, do we really want a society in which selected psychiatrists and government officials decide the validity of theological convictions and beliefs? I think not. In an increasingly secular and pluralistic society, all churches begin to play sectarian roles (Demerath and Williams, 1984:5). Cultural and legal precedents established to repress cults most likely will effect acceptable high commitment religious groups in the immediate future and eventually mainline churches as well. Ultimately, it is an issue of civil and religious liberties in an oligarchic state. The so-called solution to the "cult problem" proposed by some detractors smacks of Orwellian Big Brotherism, and would seem to leave us with a solution immanently more threatening than the problem itself (see Delgado, 1979-80; Richardson and Van Driel, 1984; Robbins, 1985b). Put in medical terms, the cure is worse than the disease. It would seem far more preferable to tolerate the unconventional beliefs and lifestyles of a few esoteric religious groups than to invite potential interference and control accompanying an expanded role of government in religious affairs. Let us hope we are left to work through the "problem" and are spared of any unwanted infringements upon our religious freedom. As Justice Louis Brandeis wrote many years ago,[5]

> Experience should teach us to be most on guard to protect liberty when the government's purposes are beneficent. Men born to freedom are naturally alert to repel invasion of their liberty by evil-minded rulers. The greatest dangers to liberty lurk in insidious encroachments by men of zeal, well-meaning but without understanding.

It is Max Weber's legacy that he understood the significance of religious innovation and expression as a counterbalance to the increasingly rational and hardened institutional fabric of Western society (1963, 1968). He painstakingly argued that secular rationalization processes foster rigid and routine forms of life that frequently prove insufficient for managing a growing state of tension, strain or suffering. Within the charismatic forces of history lie the spontaneous, the unpredictable, the creative and the genius. These forces provide an indispensable source of life to society and supply the truly revolutionary changes that shape the future. By definition, charisma does not arise in conventional forms nor express itself as traditional authority. It is unconventional, extraordinary, and unstable before routinization processes capture and tame its dynamism. Given the centrality of charismatic movements in history, one must question the conventional wisdom of those who would suppress unpopular or nontraditional religion for the "good of society."

APPENDIX A

METHODOLOGICAL PROCEDURES

A snowball sampling method was used to locate voluntary defectors. One liability of the snowball sample is that any formulated list of defectors will be partial and incomplete. Snowball sampling rests on the assumption tht the "sample eventually selected would be similar to those persons who would have been sampled if the snowball process had been allowed to continue" (Eckhardt and Ermann, 1977:253). The major disadvantage of purposive sampling is that no estimate of the risk of error can be made, based on probability. Given the nature of the population I wanted to study, and the usual restrictions of time and funding, this was a limitation I had to accept. However, it is worth noting that the matched samples of members and defectors are very similar in composition with no statistically significant differences among social background characteristics as revealed in T-tests.

Specific information about the subject matter was obtained through the use of intensive, in-depth interviews. These were designed around structured questionnaire and accomplished two purposes in the research strategy. First, direct interaction with the respondent in the interview situation created a greater sense of empathy with the individual while allowing more freedom and flexibility to gather accurate and complete details on open-ended questions (see Gordon, 1980:57-64). The opportunity to build rapport with subjects through the vehicle of the interview was a distinct advantage and one which can hardly be overstated. I found participants to be noticeably less reserved once they sensed in me an absence of the stigma often associated with cult involvement. Second, it permitted probing on structured questionnaire items when responses seemed imprecise, vague, or incomplete. Some of the most useful information in the interview was acquired when respondents were asked to elaborate upon or clarify a point. In repeated instances, an initial reply to a question failed to supply any meaningful detail and only a determined and persistent inquiry produced the information desired. In addition, my presence proved to be helpful on several occasions in which I was asked to clarify a *question* in the interview. Therefore, the chances of the subject misunderstanding items in the questionnaire were reduced significantly. In short, the exchange of information was enhanced immeasurably by this method of data collection.

The sample size for defectors was set at forty-five. The determination of size was based on two primary considerations. First, a large enough sample size was needed to accommodate an equal number of defectors from each movement, while maintaining reasonable subsample sizes. The second consideration was based on the difficult task of locating and gaining access to anonymous ex-members. While not wanting to jeopardize the adequacy of the sample for analytical purposes, I was well aware that tracking down a subpopulation of voluntary defectors could be an overwhelming project in terms of time, energy, and money. Probably the most formidable challenge posed by the research project was to design a workable blueprint within these given restraints. In an effort to balance adequate numbers for analysis with time and cost considerations, an N of forty-five was decided upon. Ideally, the sample should be larger to avoid small cell sizes in subsample breakdowns of the data. Unfortunately, however, social scientists have to live in the real world where less-than-ideal research designs are commonplace. Even the meager sample sizes garnered here represent a year and a half of field work.

Forty-five interview questionnaires were administered to current members of the three world-transforming movements to serve as a control sample. Interviews with current members were obtained with the permission of local organizational authorities of each group. Generally, it was found that the local organizations were reasonably cooperative in these efforts. It was my impression that these groups, particularly the Unification Church, had become accustomed to being approached by researchers conducting studies and seeking interviews. Thus my "intrusion" was met with little resistance. The organizations in quesion claimed they had nothing to hide and indeed, I was given the liberty of wandering freely in the centers, conducting spontaneous discussions, making inquiries, observing work cadres, attending worship services, meetings, and lectures. A schedule of interviews was arranged utilizing available members whose routine assignments placed them at the centers. Since all members are assigned in-house duties on a rotating basis I felt confident that the available pool of respondents did not represent a select group of members set aside because of a special loyalty or favored status. However, I also asked and was granted the freedom to randomly select some of the interviewees in order to deflect such a possibility. The interviews were held in vacant rooms to insure privacy, minimize the likelihood of making statements to satisfy significant others, and promote openness and candidness.

Several means were employed to generate sample members in the target group of defectors. First and foremost, posters were printed and distributed at several major college campuses in the Northeast soliciting biographical information from former members of the three religious movements studied. These were accompanied by ads placed in campus newspapers which duplicated the wording of the posters. Interested candidates were encouraged to call (collect, if necessary) the telephone numbers listed in the ads to make inquiries or arrange for an interview. The first wave of responses produced fourteen interviews and numerous secondary contacts. Some of these individuals, particularly those of whom attended the university where I conducted the research, proved to be an invaluable resource throughout the study as their deviant career "expertise" was repeatedly called upon to provide much needed information and insight.

Another method of finding sample members involved contacting several religious organizations about information concerning defectors. I was referred to a church-sponsored "half-way house" for troubled youth and an independent organization in California which collects information of new religions. These efforts resulted in three additional interviews, and they, in turn supplied four further contacts.

I also attempted to locate defectors by contacting various anticult organizations. One would suppose that these organizations would have extensive ties with ex-members. However, all my efforts produced only four interviews with *voluntary* defectors. Reasons for this became clear to me only as the research project progressed. Anticult organizations could offer only limited assistance in helping to locate voluntary defectors because most of their membership, or contact with defectors, is limited to persons who have undergone deprogramming or "rehabilitation," and, in turn, favor this type of treatment for others. Indeed, a recurring theme in their ideology is the belief that deprogramming or exit therapy is the best, if not the only, way in which individuals successfully manage to withdraw. Certainly, maintaining a surplus of ex-members who are favorably disposed to deprogramming/rehabilitation gives credibility to this argument. One must also take into account that because these organizations rely primarily on brainwashing explanations of conversion, they most likely have attracted persons with similar convictions about the importance and legitimacy of deprogramming. Consequently, limited contact and lack of knowledge about voluntary defectors has led anticult organizations to conclude that few persons leave these movements on their own. This fact was repeatedly confirmed in conversations with spokespersons of the organizations who, time and time again, expressed doubts about finding more than just a handful of voluntary defectors.

Obstacles in Fieldwork

The problem of using anticult organizations to find voluntary defectors was but one obstacle encountered in the study. I want to briefly mention a few others for the benefit of other researchers and interested readers.

A second problem encountered in the research involved the occasional refusal of ex-members to grant interviews. These persons tended to complain about being "besieged" by writers, graduate students, and reporters, and usually expressed a desire to be left alone. Though refusal to cooperate never presented itself as a major obstacle (approximately eight persons refused interviews), the partial resolution of the problem is worth recounting. In all cases where initial contact failed to gain an interview, I contacted the person who gave out the defector's name—an obvious advantage of the snowball sampling technique. The informant's aid was then enlisted in obtaining the cooperation of the potential respondent. All but one of the informants agreed to help. A few days following the request, a follow-up telephone call was made to find out 1) if the potential respondent had been reached, and 2) if he or she would be willing to talk to me. In three instances, these efforts paid off and an interview was obtained after a second contact.

A related problem warrants mentioning also. Upon attempting to make initial contact with one defector from the Hare Krishna movement, I was prevented from speaking with the person by the individual's parents. The parent answering the call was clearly suspicious of my inquiry, even though name and verifiable credentials were freely given. Based on this conversation and later discussions with sources close to the individual, it was discovered that the parents of the ex-devotee were seeking to "protect" him (he was 22 years old) from what they perceived as an unfortunate event in the young man's life. Assurances of confidentiality and anonymity of subjects did not appease the parents. A subsequent call was then made to the individual (and close friend of the ex-devotee) who originally provided the name. This person seemed familiar with the problem and assured me that she would get in touch with the defector as soon as possible. A few days later, the defector contacted me by phone to arrange for an interview. In stark contrast to attitudes exhibited by the parents, I found that the defector was more than willing to talk about his experiences. He also expressed an earnest disagreement with his parents about how his own involvement was conceptualized. This conflict of interpretation has been discussed by Beckford (1978) and suggests that even after voluntary withdrawal, some parents may be reluctant to accept the idea that their offspring were willingly involved in a "cult." The parents chose to see their son an innocent "victim" rather than a willing participant. But the defector sharply disagreed. This information proved to be very useful as the complexities of this drama unfolded. Yet, I most likely would have been denied access, had I not had the option of enlisting the aid of the informant. This provided the only means of communicating with the respondent once the normal mode of exchange was interrupted.

Another problem in the research involved the difficulty of finding defectors due to name changes. In two of the three groups examined here (the Children of God and the Hare Krishna), members were given new names to symbolize their new identity. Converts to the Children of God take names of biblical figures such as Joshua, Ezekiel, Zephaniah, and Cephas. New Krishna devotees are assigned names in Sanskrit by their guru, which may be a translation of their English name or may simply reflect a trait attributable to the devotee's personality. By virtue of the name changes, members often know each other only by the name given to them by the movement. Consequently, when an individual defects, other persons may not know or remember the actual name of the defector. The problem is compounded by the fact that members are generally encouraged not to dwell on the past, or the "old" life, so such information rarely could be learned through conversations in day-to-day living. In several cases, it was found that defectors could only identify other ex-members by their group-given name. I did not resolve the problem and mention it only that other researchers may anticipate making allowances (mostly involving time) for such obstacles in preparation for field research on new religions.

APPENDIX B

TABLES

RESPONDENTS BY GENDER.

	Defectors		Members		Total	
	%	N	%	N	%	N
Male	64.4	(29)	57.8	(26)	61.1	(55)
Female	35.6	(16)	42.2	(19)	38.9	(35)
Total	100	(45)	100	(45)	100	(90)

Table B.2 **RESPONDENTS BY RACIAL OR ETHNIC BACKGROUND.**

	Defectors		Members		Total	
	%	N	%	N	%	N
White-Anglo	97.8	(44)	80	(36)	88.9	(80)
Black	0	(0)	8.9	(4)	4.4	(4)
Hispanic	2.2	(1)	6.7	(3)	4.4	(4)
Oriental	0	(0)	4.4	(2)	2.2	(2)
Total	100	(45)	100	(45)	99.9	(90)

Table B.3 **RESPONDENTS BY AGE AT JOINING.**

	Defectors		Members		Total	
	%	N	%	N	%	N
Under 18	6.7	(3)	8.9	(4)	7.8	(7)
18-19	35.6	(16)	17.8	(8)	26.7	(24)
20-21	22.2	(10)	28.9	(13)	25.6	(23)
22-23	13.3	(6)	20.0	(9)	16.7	(15)
24-25	13.3	(6)	13.3	(6)	13.3	(12)
Over 25	8.9	(4)	11.1	(5)	10.0	(9)
Total	100	(45)	100	(45)	100.1	(90)

Table B.4	RESPONDENTS BY HIGHEST LEVEL OF EDUCATION BEFORE JOINING.					
	Defectors		Members		Total	
	%	N	%	N	%	N
Some High School	11.1	(5)	2.2	(1)	6.7	(6)
High School Graduate	8.9	(4)	22.2	(10)	15.6	(14)
Technical School	6.7	(3)	6.7	(3)	6.7	(6)
Some College	55.6	(25)	55.6	(25)	55.6	(50)
College Graduate	13.3	(6)	6.7	(3)	10.0	(9)
Some Graduate School	4.4	(2)	6.7	(3)	5.6	(5)
Total	100	(45)	100	(45)	100	(90)

Table B.5	RESPONDENTS BY SELF-DESCRIBED SOCIAL CLASS BACKGROUND.					
	Defectors		Members		Total	
	%	N	%	N	%	N
Upper	4.4	(2)	4.4	(2)	4.4	(4)
Upper middle	28.9	(13)	15.6	(7)	22.2	(20)
Middle	48.9	(22)	57.8	(26)	53.3	(48)
Lower middle	17.8	(8)	20.0	(9)	18.9	(17)
Lower	0.0	(0)	2.2	(1)	1.1	(1)
Total	100	(45)	100	(45)	99.9	(90)

Table B.6	RESPONDENTS BY PRIOR RELIGIOUS BACKGROUNDS.					
	Defectors		Members		Total	
	%	N	%	N	%	N
Catholic	44.4	(20)	37.8	(17)	41.1	(37)
Jewish	6.7	(3)	11.1	(5)	8.9	(8)
Protestant	46.7	(21)	35.6	(16)	41.1	(37)
Other	0	(0)	6.7	(3)	3.3	(3)
None	2.2	(1)	8.9	(4)	5.6	(5)
Total	100	(45)	100	(45)	100	(90)

Table B.7 **PRIOR RELIGIOUS BACKGROUND OF RESPONDENTS BY GROUP.**

	COG		HKM		UC		TOTAL	
	%	N	%	N	%	N	%	N
Catholic	43.3	(13)	40.0	(12)	40.0	(12)	41.1	(37)
Jewish	3.3	(1)	16.7	(5)	6.7	(2)	8.9	(8)
Protestant	40.0	(12)	36.7	(11)	46.7	(14)	41.1	(37)
Other	6.7	(2)	3.3	(1)	3.3	(1)	5.6	(5)
None	6.7	(2)	3.3	(1)	3.3	(1)	5.6	(5)
Total	100	(30)	100	(30)	100	(30)	100	(90)

Table B.8 **RESPONDENTS BY RELIGIOUS SEEKERSHIP.**

	Defectors		Members		Total	
	%	N	%	N	%	N
Yes	73.3	(33)	75.6	(34)	74.4	(67)
No	26.7	(12)	24.4	(11)	25.6	(23)
Total	100	(45)	100	(45)	100	(90)

NOTES

Chapter One

[1]The concentration of protest regarding totalistic lifestyles is really aimed at core members, not marginal affiliates. It is the core members who experience the highest levels of encapsulation and exhibit the most intense loyalties and devotion.

[2]The notion of "brainwashing" has difficulty as a scientific concept (Robbins and Anthony, 1980a, 1982). Thomas Szasz (1976) argues that brainwashing is a metaphor, and that one cannot really "wash a brain" any more than one can make a person "bleed" with a "cutting" remark. Some contest the use of the term in the absence of any physical coercion. But even in the face of evidence of physical coercion, the validity of the concept remains problematic, as the Patty Hearst case has shown. Dr. Walter Reich (1976) contends that psychiatry lacks the expertise and clinical experience to make reliable judgments in this area.

[3]Conway and Siegelman's recent book, *Holy Terror* (1982), is a frightening example of this attitude. Compare this later work with the earlier, *Snapping: The Epidemic of Sudden Personality Change* (1978). The authors have demonstrated a narrow understanding of church history and the role of religion in societal change (Cox, 1978; Hargrove, 1980, 1983; Miller, 1983).

[4]Recently, Barker (1985:40) has estimated that as many as 40,000 members could have left the Unification Church in the West during the 1970s.

[5]I have not included studies that employ survey or demographic research to look at religious switching, unchurched persons, or denominational losses in membership (see Caplovitz and Sherrow, 1977; Greeley, 1972, 1981; Hadaway, 1980; Hale, 1977; Hunsberger, 1980; Princeton Religious Research Center and Gallup Organization, 1978; Roof, 1981; Roozen, 1978, 1980).

[6]I refer here to "exit therapy," "intervention therapy," "exit counseling," "deprogramming," or any of a number of systematic methods designed to promote or facilitate defection. For a discussion of these see Solomon, 1981.

Chapter Two

[1]The existent literature on desocialization is remarkably thin. Goffman (1961) examines the process of "disculturation" in relation to initiation of inmates to total institutions. He purposely avoids the term desocialization, however, feeling it is "too strong" because it implies "a loss of fundamental capacities to communicate and cooperate" (1961:13). Berger and Luckman (1966) resolve the problem by distinguishing between primary and secondary socialization. The former "ends when the concept of 'generalized other' has been established in the consciousness of the individual," while the latter is an ongoing process of "further internalizations"—"socialization is never total and never finished" (1966:157-163; see also Kennedy and Kerber, 1973). Despite not using the word desocialization, they have a rather good analysis of its dynamics incorporated in a discussion of resocialization (1966:57-163). McHugh (1966) uses desocialization as an analytic concept, referring to the removal of prison subculture behavior patterns. Aside from occasional references in textbooks, the subject as a whole has been relatively ignored.

[2]The "world-transforming" concept should be understood as one which is somewhat rhetorical because of the exaggerated claims of the organizations in question. This is a feature they appear to share with a number of fundamentalist religious organizations. At least since 1980, the change that has taken place in some groups (such as the Unification Church) as they have sought to gain legitimacy in the U.S. suggests that it may be the movement, not the society, that is being transformed. The increasing emphasis on alternatives to street solicitation as the sole means of fundraising is one example (see Bromley, 1985; Richardson, 1982).

[3]For the greater part of their histories these movements have relied upon communal structures. As we move further into the 1980s, however, there appears to be some organizational changes which might alter the exclusive dependence on such forms. While the communal structure continues to play a central role in the operations of these movements, shifts in movement evolution and strategy have required the implementation of different organizational approaches. For example, the Unification Church is now experimenting with Home Church groups, in an attempt to create a place for members who cannot abandon secular responsibilities and jobs (see Barker, 1984; Beckford, 1985). This link to the surrounding secular world may allow the movement to spread its influence, or it may backfire, accelerating the process of cultural accommodation and permitting members to establish strong extra-group bonds that contribute to membership losses. Similarly, organizational changes have taken place in the Children of God/Family of Love in recent years. Moses David (1981) has encouraged smaller bands of missionary families in the massive migration to third world countries, discarding the earlier and larger communal colonies. The effects of this organizational strategy remain to be seen.

Chapter Three

[1]Kilbourne's statistical analysis of the Conway and Siegelman data has been challenged as well. See Maher and Langone, 1985.

2Funding from the National Science Foundation grant was channeled through the University of Connecticut's Research Foundation and received in the form of a pre-doctoral fellowship. The NIMH grant (#5T32MH15123-07) provided funding for revisions of the manuscript while the author was a post-doctoral fellow at Yale University.
3Deprogrammed ex-members were tied together through centralized contacts with their deprogrammers, therapists, or counselors. Anticult organizations maintain contact with deprogrammed individuals because they tended to support the brainwashing model of conversion. Indeed, many deprogrammed persons became deprogrammers themselves, or at least agreed to assist in cases where their former groups were involved. On the other hand, voluntary defectors had no such formal networks. Information tying defectors together was based on informal and typically one-time contacts or piecemeal recollections of former devotees of whom they learned of defection second hand. There was no evidence of routine or systematic communication and, to my knowledge, no formal affiliations with ex-member organizations.

Chapter Four

1Greil and Rudy's (1980) concept of "sociological cocoons" is instructive. Sociological cocoons refer to organizations whose main goal is the transformation of identity (e.g., Alcoholics Anonymous, self-help groups, religious sects, rehabilitation agencies). Through encapsulation, resocialization processes are heightened. However, encapsulation is not simply reduced to the physical, as we find in communal organizations. Greil and Rudy identify three dimensions of encapsulation: physical, social, and ideological. Some organizations may accomplish identity transformation through social and ideological encapsulation in a *noncommunal* context (Alcoholics Anonymous). Therefore, physical encapsulation can be a significant augmentative component, but not a necessary one. This is an important consideration since developments in the mid-1980s among world-transforming movements suggest a possible de-emphasis on communal structures.

2All names of participants have been changed to preserve anonymity.

3In 1981, Moses David Berg issued a mandate for all members of the Children of God to evacuate the Northern Hemisphere. He told his followers that there would likely be a nuclear holocaust in the near future. South and Central America have been popular regions of refuge. According to some members I interviewed, the Children of God have had a reasonable measure of success in these countries.

4Separations are typically much longer than seven months. All of the couples whom I interviewed had been separated for more than a year and one couple had been apart for three years.

5I was unable to obtain an interview with Catherine at the request of her husband. All of the information compiled about the couple's experience was given by Jeff. Thus, Catherine is not technically one of the eight respondents I have counted. But she is included in the seven couples I described.

6Of course, the object of the study is to show how cognitive dissonance can be managed successfully. Most members of the UFO cult remained despite disconfirmation of the predicted event. But one must take note of the defections as well. Not all members assimilate these contradictions favorably.

7However, as I show later, closeness to family before joining exhibits a significant relationship with defection. But there is no evidence to suggest that the source of disillusionment lies in unfulfilled affective needs within the group. The communal milieu offers a powerfully charged setting for developing emotional bonds and defection usually occurs in spite of, rather than as a lack of, these close-knit ties.

8The conclusion might also be true of noncommunal movements as well (see Snow and Phillips, 1980).

9The importance of "trust" in marital commitments can hardly be understated. Weiss (1975:28-32) found deterioration of trust to be a prominent aspect among failing marriages. He states, "By the time they actually separate, both husband and wife badly need the reassurance provided by a trustworthy supportive relationship" (1975:30).

Chapter Five

1See pp. 26-27.

2Coding of the third item presented a problem since initial reactions by parents sometimes changed. Thus, the respondent was asked to characterize the "predominant" attitude of one's parents over the bulk of his/her cult career.

3The contingency tables suggest there may be important interactions among variables. Thus, several different models were tested using loglinear and logit analysis to determine the effects of certain parameters upon the data (see Wright and Piper, 1986). It was found that the interaction between family closeness and parental attitudes was unclear, but that this interactive effect, plus the main effect of adolescence was important in helping to explain defection from or continued membership in these movements.

Chapter Six

1Galanter (1983:185) has observed that in the initial training phase, some individuals may even be counseled by the group to leave. These are said to occur if the person in question show signs of "psychological instability." See also Richardson, et al. 1981.

2See pp. 64-65.

3I am indebted to Myra Marx Ferree for pointing out this relationship to me.

4James Richardson was most helpful in calling my attention to possible differences in exiting modes associated with length of membership.

Chapter Seven

[1]For a better understanding of contemporary fundamentalist/evangelical or charismatic religious groups, see Ammerman, 1983; Bradfield, 1979; Dayton, 1976; Fowler, 1982; Hunter, 1983; Leibman and Wuthnow, 1983; Paloma, 1982; Quebedeaux, 1978.

[2]This is simply the Protestant "work ethic" which is still strongly embraced by evangelicals today (Fowler, 1982:26). "Born again" Christians who comprise the evangelical mainstream often emphasize service in one's occupational calling as the best way to honor God and aid humankind. Excessive focus on social action diverts people from the transforming power of Christ to involvement with political and social structures and "their age-old record of limited success at best" (Fowler, 1982:26).

[3]Given the inflated rhetoric of world-transforming movements, the similarities are even more striking than most people realize.

Chapter Eight

[1]Moreover, it would be a fundamental error not to recognize that the Army also employs "specific behavior conditioning practices." Individuals live communally in barracks, are insulated from the outside world, are subject to controls over sexual and marital lifestyles, placed in a highly authoritarian social system, and during periods of conscription, may be involuntary participants. Are these techniques of brainwashing? It would appear that the criteria for "psychological mind control" are unevenly applied.

Chapter Nine

[1]The high turnover rates indicate that the alleged brainwashing techniques are not very effective. One observer has said, "If such groups are practicing brainwashing as such, they are doing a tremendously sloppy job of it" (Sage, 1976:49). In one study, Galanter (1983) found that only 9 percent of recruits attending Moonie "work-shops" decided to join.

[2]Admittedly, the line distinguishing voluntary and involuntary "aids" to exiting (e.g., exit therapy, exit counseling, rehabilitation) have become blurred at times and remain problematic. In practice, these methods may or may not be coercive and vary widely in their implementation.

[3]At the time Lofland first published *Doomsday Cult* in 1966, the Unification Church was struggling and had achieved only a few converts. It was not until 1970 that the movement began to see large increases in their membership. "It is a fact of fundamental import," says Lofland (1979:163), ". . . that all during the turbulent social optimism of the '60s, the DPs (Moonies) did not do well at converting." Lofland attributes their success both to heightened efforts at recruitment and the changing social context of the 1970s.

[4]Szasz (1984:180) suggests, for example, that being a "born-again Christian" could easily be interpreted as a form of mental illness. If the contention was taken literally by psychiatrists, ". . . then the claim of having been born more than once [c]ould be called a delusion symptomatic of a psychosis."

[5]Quoted in Nisbet (1979:16).

BIBLIOGRAPHY

Aberle, David
1966   *The Peyote Religion Among the Navaho.*
       Chicago: Aldine.

Ammerman, Nancy
1983   *The Fundamentalist Worldview: Ideology
       and Social Structure in an Independent
       Fundamentalist Church.* Ph.D. Disserta-
       tion, Yale University.

Babbie, Earl
1975   *The Practice of Social Research.* Belmont:
       Wadsworth.

Barker, Eileen
1983a "Resistible Coercion: The Significance of
       Failure Rates in conversion and commit-
       ment to the Unification Church." In Dick
       Anthony, Jacob Needleman, and Thomas
       Robbins (eds.), *Conversion, Coercion and
       Commitment in New Religious Movements.*
       New York: Crossroads Press.
1983b "Supping With the Devil." *Sociological
       Analysis* 44(3):197-206.
1984   *The Making of a Moonie: Choice or Brain-
       washing?* New York: Basil Blackwell.
1985   "New Religious Movements: Yet Another
       Great Awakening?" pp. 36-57 in Phillip E.
       Hammond (ed.) *The Sacred in a Secular
       Age.* Berkeley: University of California.

Becker, Howard S.
1960   "Notes on the Concept of Commitment."
       American Journal of Sociology 66:32-40.

Beckford, James A.
1978   "Through the Looking-Glass and Out the
       Other Side: Withdrawal from Reverend
       Moon's Unification Church." *Archives de
       Sciences Sociales des Religions* 45:95-
       116.
1981   "Conversion and Apostasy: Antithesis or
       Complementarity?" Paper presented at
       Conference on "Conversion, Coercion,
       and Commitment in the New Religions,"
       Berkeley, California, June 11-14.
1982   "A Typology of Family Responses to a New
       Religious Movement," pp. 41-56 in Flor-
       ence Kaslow and Marvin B. Sussman
       (eds.), *Cults and the Family.* Boston: Ha-
       worth Press.
1983   "Some Questions About the Relationship
       Between Scholars and the New Religious
       Movements." *Sociological Analysis*
       44(3):189-196.
1985   *Cult Controversies: The Societal Response
       to the New Religious Movements.* London:
       Tavistock.

Bell, Daniel
1976   *The Cultural Contradictions of Capitalism.*
       New York: Basic Books.

Bellah, Robert N.
1976   "New Religious Consciousness and the
       Crisis in Modernity," pp. 333-352 in
       Charles Y. Glock and Robert N. Bellah
       (eds.), *The New Religious Consciousness.*
       Berkeley: University of California.

Berg, Moses David
1973   "The Comet Comes!" No. 283. Children of
       God.
1974   "The Comet's Tale." No. 295. Children of
       God.
1976   *The Basic Mo Letters.* Geneva: Children of
       God.
1981   *Family International News.* No. 40. Zurich,
       Switzerland: Family of Love.

Berger, Peter L.
1978   *Facing Up to Modernity.* New York: Basic
       Books.

Berger, Peter L. and Thomas Luckmann
1966   *The Social Construction of Reality.* Garden
       City, N.Y.: Doubleday.

Berger, Peter L. and Richard Neuhaus
1976   *Against the World for the World.* New York:
       Seabury.

Bergin, A. E.
1980   "Psychotherapy and Religious Values."
       *Journal of Consulting and Clincial Psychol-
       ogy* 48:95-105.

Bird, Frederick and Bill Reimer
1982   "Participation Rates in New Religious and
       Para-Religious Movments." *Journal for the
       Scientific Study of Religion* 21(1):1-14.

Blau, Peter M.
1963   *Dynamics of Bureaucracy: A Study of Inter-
       personal Relationships in Two Governmen-
       tal Agencies.* Chicago: University of Chi-
       cago.

Bloch, Sidney and Peter Reddaway
1977   *Psychiatric Terror: How Soviet Psychiatry is
       Used to Suppress Dissent.* New York: Basic
       Books.

Bradfield, Cecil D.
1979   *Neo-Pentecostalism: A Sociological Study.*
       Washington: University Press of America.

Brinkerhoff, Merlin B. and Katheryn L. Burke
1980   "Disaffiliation: Some notes on 'Falling from
       the Faith.' " *Sociological Analysis* 41:41-
       54.

Bromley, David G.
1985   "Financing the Millennium: The Economic
       Structure of the Unificationist Movement."
       Journal for the Scientific Study of Religion
       24(3):253-274.

Bromley, David G. and Anson D. Shupe
1980   *"Moonies" in America: Cult, Church, Cru-
       sade.* Beverly Hills: Sage.
1980   "Financing the New Religions: A Re-
       source Mobilization Approach." *Journal for
       the Scientific Study of Religion* 19(3):227-
       238.

Bromley, David G. and James T. Richardson
1983   *The Deprogramming/Brainwashing Contro-
       versy: Sociological, Psychological, Legal
       and Historical Perspectives.* New York:
       Edwin Mellen.

Bromley, David G., Anson D. Shupe and Donna Oliver
1982   "Perfect Families: Visions of the Future in
       New Religious Movements,' pp. 119-130 in
       Florence Karlow and Marvin B. Sussman

(eds.), *Cults and the Family.* New York: Haworth.

Bromley, David G., Anson D. Shupe and J. C. Ventimiglia
1983 "The Role of Anecdotal Atrocities in the Social Construction of Evil," pp. 139-160 in David G. Bromley and James T. Richardson (eds.) *The Brainwashing/Deprogramming Controversy.* New York: Edwin Mellen.

Cantril, Hadley
1963 *The Psychology of Social Movements.* New York: Wiley and Sons.

Carrol, J. and B. Bauer
1979 "Suicide Training in the Moon Cult." *New West* (January 29): 62-3.

Caplovitz, David and Fred Sherrow
1977 *The Religious Dropouts: Apostasy Among College Graduates.* Beverly Hills: Sage.

Chiriboga, D. A. and M. Thurner
1980 "Marital Life-styles and Adjustments to Separation." *Journal of Divorce* 3 (Summer):379-390.

Clark, John
1979 "Cults." *Journal of the American Medical Association* 242:279-281.

Clark, John, Michael D. Langone, Robert Schacter and Roger C. G. Daly
1981 *Destructive Cult Conversion: Theory, Research and Practice.* Weston, MA.: American Family Foundation.

Clarke, Juanna
1979 "Medicalization and Sacralization." Paper presented to Association of the Sociology of Religion, Boston.

Coleman, James S.
1970 "Social Inventions." *American Journal of Sociology,* 49:163-173.

Conrad, Peter and Joseph W. Schneider
1980 *Deviance and Medicalization.* London: Mosby.

Conway, Flo and Jim Siegelman
1978 *Snapping: The Epidemic of Sudden Personality Change.* New York: J. B. Lippincott.
1982 *Holy Terror.* Garden City, NY: Doubleday.

Coser, Lewis A.
1974 *Greedy Institutions: Patterns of Undivided Commitment.* New York: Free Press.

Cox, Harvey
1978 "Myths Sanctioning Religious Persecution," pp. 3-10 in M. Darrol Bryant and Herbert Richardson (eds.), *A Time for Consideration.* New York: Edwin Mellen.

Cross, Whitney R.
1950/ *The Burned-Over District: The Social and*
1982 *Intellectual History of Enthusiastic Religion in Western New York, 1800-1850.* Ithaca, NY: Cornell University Press.

Cuddihy, John
1975 *The Ordeal of Civility.* New York: Basic Books.

Daner, Francine
1976 *The American Children of Krsna: A Study of the Hare Krsna Movement.* New York: Holt, Rinehart and Winston.

Davis, Rex and James T. Richardson
1976 "The Organization and Functioning of the Children of God," *Sociological Analysis* 37:321-39.

Dayton, Donald
1976 *Discovering an Evangelical Heritage.* New York: Harper & Row.

Dearman, Marion
1974 "Christ and Conformity: A Study of Pentecostal Values," *Journal for the Scientific Study of Religion* 13:437-454.

Delgado, Richard
1977 "Religious Totalism: Gentle and Ungentle Persuasion," *Southern California Law Review* 15:1-100.
1979-80 "Religious Totalism as Slavery." *New York University Review of Law and Social Change* 9:1-34.
1980 "Limits of Proselytizing," *Society* 17:25-33.

Demerath, J. N. III and Rhys H. Williams
1984 "A Mythical Past and Uncertain Future." *Society* 21(4):3-10.

Doress Irvin and Jack N. Porter
1981 "Kids in Cults," pp. 297-302 in Thomas Robbins and Dick Anthony (eds.), *In Gods We Trust: New Patterns of Religious Pluralism in America.* New Brunswick, NJ: Transaction.

Ebaugh, Helen Rose Fuchs
1977 *Out of the Cloister: A Study of Organizational Dilemmas.* Austin: University of Texas.

Eckhardt, Kenneth and M. David Ermann
1977 *Social Research Methods.* New York: Random House.

Edwards, Christopher
1979 *Crazy for God.* Englewood Cliffs, NJ: Prentice-Hall.

Eisenstadt, Shmuel
1964 "Institutionalization and Change," *American Sociological Review* 64:115-127.

Enroth, Ronald
1977 *Extremist Cults, Youth, and Brainwashing.* Kentwood, MI: Zondervan.

Federico, Joseph
1979 "The Marital Termination Period of the Divorce Adjustment Process." *Journal of Divorce* 3(2):93-106.

Ferree, Myers Marx and Frederick D. Miller
1985 "Mobilization and Meaning: Toward An Integration of Social Movements." *Sociological Inquiry* 55:38-51.

Festinger, Leon
1957 *A Theory of Cognitive Dissonance.* Evanston, IL: Row, Peterson, and Company.

Fichter, Joseph H.
1983 "Family and Religion Among the Moonies: A Descriptive Analysis," pp. 289-304 in William V. D'Antonio and Joan Aldous (eds.), *Families and Religions: Conflict and Change in Modern Society.* Beverly Hills: Sage.

Flacks, Richard
1970   *Youth and Social Change.* New York: Markham.

Foster, Lawrence
1981   *Religion and Sexuality: Three American Communal Experiments in the Nineteenth Century.* New York: Oxford University Press.

Fowler, Robert Booth
1982   *A New Engagement: Evangelical Political Thought, 1966-1976.* Grand Rapids, MI: Eerdmans.

Frame, Randy
1983   "And Now—Deprogramming Christians is Taking Place." *Christianity Today* April 22.

Fromm, Eric
1950   *Psychoanalysis and Religion.* New Haven: Yale University Press.

Galanter, Marc
1983a   "Group Induction Techniques in a Charismatic Sect," pp. 182-193 in David G. Bromley and James T. Richardson (eds.), *The Brainwashing/Deprogramming Controversy: Sociological, Psychological, Legal and Historical Perspectives.* New York: Edwin Mellen.

1983b   "Unification Church ('Moonie') Dropouts: Psychological Readjustment After Leaving a Charismatic Religious Group." *American Journal of Psychiatry* 140:984-89.

Galper, Marvin F.
1976   "The Cult Indoctrinee: A New Clinical Syndrome." Paper presented to the Tampa-St. Petersburg Psychiatric Society, Tampa, FL.

1982   "The Cult Phenomenon: Behavioral Science Perspectives Applied to Therapy," pp. 141-150 in Florence Kaslow and Marvin B. Surrman (eds.) *Cults and Family.* New York: Haworth.

Gamson, William A.
1975   *The Strategy of Social Protest.* Homewood, IL: Dorsey.

Gerlach, Luther P. and Virginia Hine
1970   *People, Power, Change: Movements of Social Transformation.* Indianapolis: Bobbs-Merrill.

Goffman, Erving
1961   *Asylums.* Garden City, NY: Doubleday Anchor Books.

Goode, William J.
1956   *After Divorce.* Glencoe, IL: Free Press.

Gordon, Raymond L.
1980   *Interviewing: Strategy, Techniques, and Tactics.* Homewood, IL: Dorsey.

Greeley, Andrew
1972   *The Denominational Society: A Sociological Approach to the Study of Religion in America.* Glenview, IL: Scott, Foresman.

1981   "Religious Musical Chairs," pp. 101-126 in Thomas Robbins and Dick Anthony (eds.), *In God We Trust: New Patterns of Religious Pluralism in America.* New Brunswick, NJ: Transaction.

Greil, Arthur L. and David R. Rudy
1980   "Sociological Cocoons: Organizations for the Transformation of Identity." Paper presented at the annual meetings of the Society for the Scientific Study of Religion, Cincinnati, Ohio.

Gross, M. L.
1978   *The Psychological Society:* New York: Random House.

Hadaway, C. Kirk
1980   "Denominational Switching and Religiosity," *Reveiw of Religious Research* 21:451-461.

Hammond, Phillip and David G. Bromley
Forthcoming:
        The Future of New Religions. Macon, GA: Mercer University.

Hargrove, Barbara
1979   *The Sociology of Religion.* Arlington Heights, IL: AHM Publishers.

1980   "Evil Eyes and Religious Choices." *Society* 3:20-24.

1983   "Social Sources and Consequences of the Brainwashing Controversy," pp. 299-308 in David G. Bromley and James T. Richardson (eds.) *The Brainwashing/Deprogramming Controversy.* New York: Edwin Mellen.

Hale, J. Russell
1977   *Who are the Unchurched?* Washington, D.C.: Glenmary Research Center.

Heirich, Max
1977   "Change of Heart: A Test of Some Widely Held Theories About Religious Conversion," *American Journal of Sociology* 83:653-680.

Hillery, George A.
1981   "Freedom, Love, and Community: An Outline of a Theory," pp. 303-3236 in Thomas Robbins and Dick Anthony (eds.) *In Gods We Trust: New Patterns of Religious Pluralism in America.* New Brunswick, NJ: Transaction.

Horowitz, Irving Louis
1978   *Science, Sin and Scholarship: The Politics of Reverend Moon and the Unification Church.* Cambridge: MIT Press.

1983   "Symposium on Scholarship and Sponsorship: Universal Standards, Not Uniform Beliefs." *Sociological Analysis* 44(3):179-182.

HSA-UWC
1975   *Leadership Training Manual.* Tarrytown, NY.

Hunsberger, Bruce
1980   "A Reexamination of Antecedents of Apostasy," *Review of Religious Research* 21:158-170.

Hunter, James D.
1983   *American Evangelicalism: Conservative Religion and the Quandary of Modernity.* New Brunswick: Rutgers University Press.

Jacobs, Janet
1984   "The Economy of Love in Religious Commitment: The Deconversion of Women from Non-Traditional Religious Movements." *Journal for the Scientific Study of Religion* 23(2):155-171.

Johnson, Benton
1961 "Do Holiness Sects Socialize in Dominant Values?", *Social Forces* 39:309-316.

Jorstad, Erling
1981 *Evangelicals in the White House: The Cultural Maturation of Born Again Christianity, 1960-1981.* New York: Edwin Mellen.

Jud, Gerald, G. Burch and T. Mills
1970 *Ex-Pastors: Why Men Leave the Ministry.* Philadelphia: Pilgrim Press.

Judah, J. Stillson
1974a *Hare Krishna and the Counterculture.* San Francisco: Josey-Bass.
1974b "The Hare Krishna Movement," pp. 617-645 in Irving Zaretsky and Mark P. Leone (eds.), *Religious Movements in Contemporary America.* Princeton: Princeton University Press.
1978 "New Religions and Religious Liberty," pp. 201-208 in Jacob Needleman and George Baker (eds.) *Understanding the New Religions.* New York: Seabury.

Kanter, Rosabeth Moss
1968 "Commitment and Social Organization: A Study of Commitment Mechanisms." *American Sociological Review* 33(4):499-517.
1972 *Commitment and Community: Communes and Utopias in Sociological Perspective.* Cambridge: Harvard University Press.

Kelly, Dean
1977 "Deprogramming and Religious Liberty," *Civil Liberties Review* 4,2:23-33.

Kennedy, Daniel B. and August Kerber
1973 *Resocialization: An American Experiment.* New York: Behavioral Publications.

Kenniston, Kenneth
1971 *Youth and Dissent.* New York: Harcourt, Brace and Co.
1977 *All Our Children: The American Family Under Seige.* New York: Harcourt, Brace, Jovanovich.

Kephart, William
1982 *Extraordinary Groups: The Sociology of Unconventional Lifestyles.* (Second edition). New York: St. Martins.

Kilbourne, Brock
1983 "The Conway and Siegelman Claims Against Religious Cults: An Assessment of their Data." *Journal for the Scientific Study of Religion.* 22(4):380-85.

Kilbourne, Brock and James T. Richardson
1984 "Psychotherapy and New Religions in a Pluralistic Society." *American Psychologist* 39(3):237-251.

LeMoult, John
1978 "Deprogramming Members of Religious Sects." *Fordham Law Review* 46:599-634.

Levine, Edward M.
1980 "Deprogramming Without Tears." *Society* 2:34-38.

Levine, Saul
1984 *Radical Departures: Desperate Detours to Growing Up.* New York: Harcourt, Brace, Jovanovich.

Levinger, George and Oliver C. Moles
1979 *Divorce and Separation: Context, Causes, and Consequences.* New York: Basic Books.

Liebman, Charles S.
1983 "Extremism as a Religious Norm." *Journal for the Scientific Study of Religion* 22(1):75-86.

Liebman, Robert C. and Robert Wuthnow
1983 *The New Christian Right.* New York: Aldine.

Lifton, Robert J.
1961 *Thought Reform and the Psychology of Totalism.* New York: W. W. Norton.

Lofland, John
1977 *Doomsday Cult.* Enlarged Edition. New York: Irvington.
1979 "White Hot Mobilization: Strategies of a Millenarian Movement," pp. 157-166 in Mayer N. Zald and John D. McCarthy (eds.), *The Dynamics of Social Movements.* Cambridge: Winthrop.

London, P.
1964 *The Modes and Morals of Psychotherapy.* New York: Holt, Rhinehart and Winston.

Luckmann, Thomas
1967 *The Invisible Religion.* New York: McMillan.

MacCollam, Joel A.
1979 *Carnival of Souls.* New York: Seabury.

Maher, Brendon A. and Michael D. Langone
1985 "Kilbourne on Conway and Siegelman: A Statistical Critique." *Journal for the Scientific Study of Religion* 24(3):325-26.

Marx, Gary T.
1979 "External Efforts to Damage or Facilitate Social Movements: Some Patterns, Explanations, Outcomes, and Complications," pp. 94-125 in Mayer N. Zald and John D. McCarthy (eds.), *The Dynamics of Social Movements.* Cambridge: Winthrop.

Marx, John and David Ellison
1975 "Sensitivity Training and Communes: Contemporary Quests for Community." *Pacific Sociological Review* 18:442-60.

Mauss, Armand L.
1969 "Dimensions of Religious Defection." *Review of Religious Research* 10:128-35.

McCarthy, John D. and Mayer N. Zald
1977 "Resource Mobilization and Social Movements: A Partial Theory." *American Journal of Sociology* 82:1212-1239.

Mead, G. H.
1934 *Mind, Self and Society.* Chicago: University of Chicago.

McHugh, Peter
1966 "Social Disintegration as a Prerequisite to Resocialization." *Social Forces* 44:355-63.

McLoughlin, William G.
1978 *Revivals, Awakenings and Reform.* Chicago: University of Chicago.

Miller, Jesse
1979 "The Unification of Hypnotic Techniques by Religious and Therapy Cults." Paper presented to the International Society of Political Psychology.

Miller, Donald E.
    1983   "Deprogramming in Historical Perspective," pp. 15-28 in David G. Bromley and James T. Richardson (eds.), *The Brainwashing/Deprogramming Controversy: Sociological, Psychological, Legal and Historical Perspectives.* New York: Edwin Mellen.

Minnery, Tom and Kenneth Kantzer
    1982   "It's Too Soon to Quit!," pp. 10-11 in *Christianity Today*, December 17.

Niebuhr, H. R.
    1929   *The Social Sources of Denominationalism.* New York: Meridian.

Nisbet, Robert
    1979   "The Future of the University," pp. 303-326 in S. M. Lipset (ed.), *The Third Century.* Chicago: University of Chicago.

Oberschall, Anthony
    1973   *Social Conflict and Social Movements.* Englewood Cliffs, NJ: Prentice-Hall.

Paloma, Margaret
    1982   *The Charismatic Movement: Is There a New Pentecost?* Boston: Twayne.

Patrick, Ted and Tom Dulack
    1976   *Let Our Children Go.* New York: E. P. Dutton.

Pavlos, Andrew J.
    1982   *The Cult Experience.* Westport, CT: Greenwood.

Princeton Religious Research Center and Gallup Organization
    1978   *The Unchurched American.* Princeton, N.J.

Pritchett, W. Douglas
    1985   *The Children of God/Family of Love: An Annotated Bibliography.* New York: Garland.

Prus, Robert C.
    1976   "Religious Recruitment and the Management of Dissonance." *Sociological Inquiry* 46:127-134.

Quebedeaux, Richard
    1978   *The Worldly Evangelicals.* New York: Harper & Row.

Rambo, Lewis R.
    1981   "Current Research on Religious Conversion." *Religious Studies Review* Oct.:1-96.

Reich, Walter
    1976   "Brainwashing, Psychiatry and the Law." *Psychiatry* 39:138-147.

Richardson, James T.
    1977a   *Conversion Careers: In and Out of the New Religions.* Beverly Hills: Sage.
    1977b   "Types of Conversion and 'Conversion Careers' in New Religious Movements." Paper presented at the annual meeting of the American Association for the Advancement of Science, Denver, Colo.
    1982   "Financing the New Religions: Comparative and Theoretical Perspectives." *Journal for the Scientific Study of Religion* 21(3):255-267.

Richardson, James T. and M. T. V. Reidy
    1980   "Form and Fluidity in Two Contemporary Glossalalic Movements." *Annual Review of the Social Sciences of Religion* Vol. 4:183-220.

Richardson, James T. and Mary Stewart
    1977   "Conversion Process Models and the Jesus Movement," pp. 24-42 in James T. Richardson (ed.), *Conversion Careers.* Beverly Hills: Sage.

Richardson, James T., Mary Stewart and Robert B. Simmonds
    1979   *Organized Miracles: A Study of a Contemporary, Youth Communal, Fundamentalist Organization.* New Brunswick, NJ: Transaction.

Richardson, James T., Jan van der Lans and Frans Derk
    1981   "Voluntary Disaffiliation, Expulsion and Deprogramming: An Analysis of Ways of Leaving Social Groups." Paper presented at the annual meeting of the Association for the Sociology of Religion, Toronto, Canada, August.

Richardson, James T. and Rex Davis
    1983   "Experiential Fundamentalism: Revisions of Orthodoxy in the Jesus Movement." *Journal of the American Academy of Religion* (3):397-425.

Richardson, James T. and Baron Van Driel
    1984   "Public Support for Anti-cult Legislation." *Journal for the Scientific Study of Religion* 23(4):412-19.

Richardson, Herbert
    1980   *New Religions and Mental Health.* New York: Edwin Mellen.

Rieff, Philip
    1966   *The Triumph of the Therapeutic: Uses of Faith After Freud.* New York: Harper & Row.

Robbins, Thomas
    1979   " 'Cults,' and the Therapeutic State." *Social Policy* 10:42-46.
    1981   "Church, State and Cult." *Sociological Analysis* 42:209-226.
    1983   "The Beach is Washing Away." *Sociological Analysis* 44(3):207-214.
    1984   "Constructing Cultist Mind Control." *Sociological Analysis* 45(3):241-256.
    1985a   "Nuts, Sluts, and Converts: Studying Religious Groups as a Social Problem." *Sociological Analysis* 46(2):171-178.
    1985b   "Government Regulatory Powers and Church Autonomy: Deviant Groups as Test Cases." *Journal for the Scientific Study of Religion* 24(3):237-252.

Robbins, Thomas and Dick Anthony
    1978   "New Religions, Families, and Brainwashing." *Society* May/June: 77-83.
    1980a   "The Limits of Coercive Persuasion as an Explanation for Conversion to Authoritarian Sects," *Political Psychology* 2:27-37.
    1980b   "Cults vs. Shrinks: The Control of Religious Movements," pp. 48-64 in Herbert Richardson (ed.) *New Religions and Mental Health.* New York: Edwin Mellen.
    1981   *In Gods We Trust: New Patterns of Religious Pluralism in America.* New Brunswick, NJ: Transaction.
    1982   "Deprogramming, Brainwashing, and the Medicalization of Deviant Religious Groups." *Social Problems* 39(3):283-297.

Robbins, Thomas, William Shepherd and James McBride
1985   *Cults, Culture and the Law: Perspectives on New Religious Movements.* Baltimore: Scholars Press.

Robertson, Roland
1967   "The Salvation Army: The Persistence of Sectarianism," pp. 49-105 in Bryan Wilson (ed.), *Patterns of Sectarianism.* London: Heineman.
1985   "Scholarship, Partisanship, Sponsorship and the 'Moonie Problem': A Comment." *Sociological Analysis* 46(2):179-184.

Roof, Wade Clark
1981   "Alienation and Apostasy," pp. 87-100 in Thomas Robbins and Dick Anthony (eds.), *In Gods We Trust: New Patterns of Religious Pluralism in America.*

Roozen, David A.
1978   *The Churched and Unchurched American: A Comparative Profile.* Washington, D.C.: Glenmary.
1980   "Church Dropouts: Changing Patterns of Disengagement and Reentry." *Review of Religious Research* 21:427-450.

Ruby, Walter
1985   "Cults: Is the Tide Turning?" *Hadassah Magazine* (May):20-23.

Sage, Wayne
1976   "The War on Cults." *Human Behavior* (Oct.):40-49.

San Giovanni, Lucinda
1978   *Ex-Nuns: A Study of Emergent Role Passage.* Norwood, NJ: Ablex.

Schein, Edgar, Inge Schneier and Curtis H. Barker
1961   *Coercive Persuasion.* New York: W. W. Norton.

Selengut, Charles
1985   "The New Converts: Emerging Patterns of Apostasy in American Judaism." Paper presented to annual meeting of the American Sociological Association, Washington, D.C.

Shapiro, Eli
1977   "Destructive Cultism." *American Family Physician* 15(February):80-83.

Shepherd, William C.
1983   "Constitutional Law and Marginal Religions," pp. 258-266 in David G. Bromley and James T. Richardson (eds.), *The Brainwashing/Deprogramming Controversy: Sociological, Psychological, Legal and Historical Perspectives.* New York: Edwin Mellen.
1985   *To Secure the Blessings of Liberty: American Constitutional Law and the New Religious Movements.* Baltimore: Scholars Press.

Shupe, Anson D. and David G. Bromley
1979   "The Moonies and the Anti-Cultists: Movement and Countermovement in Conflict." *Sociological Analysis* 40:325-334.
1980   *The New Vigilantes: Deprogrammers, Anti-Cultists and the New Religions.* Beverly Hills: Sage.

Siegleman, Jim and Flo Conway
1979   "Playboy Interview: Ted Patrick." *Playboy* (March):53ff.

Simmel, George
1950   *The Sociology of George Simmel,* translated and edited by Kurt Wolff. New York: Free Press.

Simpson, Ida Harper and Richard L. Simpson
1981   *Research in the Sociology of Work.* Greenwich: JAI Press.

Singer, Margaret Thaler
1979   "Coming Out of the Cults." *Psychology Today,* December(8):72-82.

Skonovd, L. Norman
1981   *Apostasy: The Process of Defection From Religious Totalism.* Ph.D Dissertation. Ann Arbor, MI: University Microfilms International.

Slater, Philip E.
1963   "On Social Regression." *American Sociological Review* 28:339-364.

Smelser, Neil
1962   *Theory of Collective Behavior.* New York: Free Press.

Smith, H. W.
1975   *Strategies of Social Research.* Englewood Cliffs, NJ: Prentice-Hall.

Snow, David A. and Cynthia L. Phillips
1980   "The Lofland-Stark Conversion Model: A Critical Assessment." *Social Problems* 27:430-47.

Snow, David and Richard Machelek
1982   "On the Presumed Fragility of Unconventional Beliefs." *Journal for the Scientific Study of Religion* 21:15-25.

Solomon, Trudy
1981   "Integrating the 'Moonie' Experience: A Survey of Ex-Members of the Unification Church," pp. 275-296 in Thomas Robbins and Dick Anthony (eds.), *In Gods We Trust: New Patterns of Religious Pluralism in America.* New Brunswick, NJ: Transaction.

Spanier, Graham B. and Robert F. Casto
1979   "Adjustment to Separation and Divorce," pp. 211-227 in George Levinger and Oliver C. Moles (eds.), *Divorce and Separation: Context, Causes, and Consequences.*

Stark, Rodney and William Sims Bainbridge
1981   "Secularization and Cult Formation in the Jazz Age." *Journal for the Scientific Study of Religion* 20:360-373.

Szasz, Thomas
1970   *Ideology and Insanity: Essays on the Psychiatric Dehumanization of Man.* Garden City, NY: Doubleday.
1974   *The Myth of Mental Illness: Foundations of a Theory of Personal Conduct.* Revised edition. New York: Harper & Row.
1976   "Some Call it Brainwashing." *New Republic* March 6:10-12.
1984   *The Therapeutic State: Psychiatry in the Mirror of Current Events.* Buffalo, NY: Prometheus.

Testa, Bart
1978   "Making Crime Seem Natural: News and Deprogramming," pp. 41-81 in M. Darrol Bryant and Herbert Richardson (eds.), *A Time for Consideration.* New York: Edwin Mellen.

Thompson, Linda and Graham B. Spanier
1983   "The End of Marriage and Acceptance of Marital Termination." *Journal of Marriage and the Family* 45(1):103-113.

Tilly, Charles
1978   *From Mobilization to Revolution.* Reading, MA: Addison-Wesley.

Toch, Hans
1965   *The Social Psychology of Social Movements.* Indianapolis: Bobbs-Merrill.

Travisano, Richard V.
1981   "Alternation and Conversion as Qualitatively Different Transformations," pp. 237-248 in Gregory P. Stone and Harvey Farberman (eds.), *Social Psychology Through Symbolic Interaction.* New York: John Wiley and Sons.

Turner, Ralph H. and Lewis M. Killian
1957   *Collective Behavior.* Englewood Cliffs, NJ: Prentice-Hall.

Underwood, Barbara and Betty Underwood
1979   *Hostage to Heaven.* New York: Potter.

Ungerleider, J. Thomas and David K. Wellisch
1979   "Coercive Persuasion (Brainwashing), Religious Cults, and Deprogramming." *American Journal of Psychiatry* 136 (March):279-282.
1983   "The Programming (Brainwashing)/Deprogramming Controversy," pp. 187-213 in David G. Bromley and James T. Richardson (eds.), *The Brainwashing/Deprogramming Controversy: Sociological, Psychological, Legal and Historical Perspectives.* New York: Edwin Mellen.

Van Maanen, John and Edgar H. Schein
1979   "Toward a Theory of Organizational Socialization," pp. 187-213 in Barry M. Shaw (ed.), *Research in Organizational Behavior.* Greenwich, CT: JAI.

Vitz, Paul
1977   *Psychology as Religion: The Cult of Self Worship.* Grand Rapids, MI: Eerdmans.

Verdier, Paul
1977   *Brainwashing and the Cults.* Redondo Beach, CA: Insitute of Behavioral Conditioning.

Wallis, Roy A.
1976   "Observations on the Children of God." *Sociological Review* 24 (November):807-829.
1978   "Recruiting Christian Manpower." *Society* (May/June):72-74.
1979   *Salvation and Protest: A Study of Social and Religious Movements.* New York: St. Martins.
1983   "Religion, Reason, and Responsibility." *Sociological Analysis* 44(3):215-220.

Weber, Max
1958   *The Protestant Ethic and the Spirit of Capitalism.* New York: Scribners.
1963   *The Sociology of Religion.* Translated by Ephraim Fischoff. Boston: Beacon.
1968   *Max Weber on Charisma and Institution Building.* Edited by S. N. Eisenstadt. Chicago: University of Chicago.

Weiss, Robert S.
1975   *Marital Separation.* New York: Basic Books.
1979   "The Emotional Impact of Marital Separation," pp. 201-210 in George Levinger and Oliver C. Moles (eds.), *Divorce and Separation: Context, Causes, and Consequences.* New York: Basic Books.

Wilson, Bryan R.
1983   "Sympathetic Detachment and Disinterested Involvement." *Sociological Analysis* 44(3):183-188.

Wilson, John
1973   *Introduction to Social Movements.* New York: Basic Books.

Wright, Stuart A.
1981   "Secularization, Unconventional Movements and Religious Dissent." Paper presented at the annual meetings of the Southwestern Social Science Association, Dallas, TX, March.
1983   "Defection from New Religious Movements: A Test of Some Theoretical Propositions," pp. 106-121 in James T. Richardson and David G. Bromley (eds.), *The Brainwashing/Deprogramming Controversy: Sociological, Psychological, Legal and Historical Perspectives.* New York: Edwin Mellen.
1984   "Post-Involvement Attitudes of Voluntary Defectors From Controversial New Religious Movements." *Journal for the Scientific Study of Religion* 23(2):172-182.
1987   "Social Movement Decline and Transformation: Cults in the '80s." Paper presented at the annual meeting of the Southwestern Social Science Association, Dallas, TX, March.

Wright, Stuart A. and Elizabeth S. Piper
1986   "Families and Cults: Familial Factors Related to Youth Leaving or Remaining in Deviant Religious Groups." *Journal of Marriage and the Family* 48(1):15-25.

Wuthnow, Robert
1976   *The Consciousness Reformation.* Berkeley: University of California.

Zablocki, Benjamin
1980   *Alienation and Charisma.* New York: Free Press.

Zald, Mayer and Roberta Ash
1966   "Social Movement Organization: Growth, Decay, and Change." *Social Forces* 44:327-41.

Zald, Mayer and John D. McCarthy
1979   *The Dynamics of Social Movements.* Cambridge: Winthrop.

Zygmunt, Joseph F.
1970   "Prophetic Failure and Chiliastic Identity: The Case of Jehovah's Witnesses." *American Journal of Sociology* 75:926-948.

NAME INDEX

SUBJECT INDEX